BACKWOODS GIRL

Little Girl in Hen Valley

Mountain Life in Tennessee in the Early 1900s

By
Ruth Risetter Watson

Illustrations by Martha Raleigh Winsten

TEACH Services, Inc.
Brushton, New York

**PRINTED IN
THE UNITED STATES OF AMERICA**

2008 09 10 11 12 · 5 4 3 2 1

Copyright © 2008 TEACH Services, Inc.
ISBN-13: 978-1-57258-487-7
ISBN-10: 1-57258-487-4
Library of Congress Control Number: 2007910393

Published by

TEACH Services, Inc.
www.TEACHServices.com

CONTENTS

"In her book, *Backwoods Girl from Hen Valley*, Ruth Watson has captured the mood and has accurately described the people and the land of eastern Tennessee in the 1920s. I thoroughly enjoyed reading the book and found myself often laughing and reminiscing about both the people and the incidents that she wrote so well about. I would highly recommend this book to anyone who is interested in a factual, historical, and often humorous glimpse into the daily lives of country people during this time in American History."—C. S. Harvey Jr., Oliver Springs Historical Society

"Ruth Watson's nostalgic story of her childhood in the depression world of the 30s mixes spontaneous innocence with the quiet Christian faith of her family. Simple pleasures, suspense involving moonshining, and compassion with love for others climaxes in the conversion of several neighbors. This charming story with a golden thread of faith touches the readers heart with its entertaining and delightful insights into human nature."—Marilyn Morgan

"Ruth shares her family's true story of life in the late 1920s in Tennessee. This lovely story follows the family through sickness, storm, and the sometimes difficult choices a family must make. It is a welcome story of witness and faith."—Jean Boonstra

"With the same charm found in *Little House on the Prairie*, Ruth Watson vividly creates the world of an young girl and her family living during the depression period. Her descriptive way of writing brings to life the exciting adventures and challenges this family face. Not only does this book capture the heart of today's young reader, it also affirms their faith as these values are woven throughout the story line. Uplifting and inspiring, Ruth Watson has brought us a classic that leaves you wishing it wouldn't end."—Judy Aitken

FOREWORD

When my parents moved to east Tennessee in 1927 for health reasons, their primary goal was to build a church for God. I was a child of about four at the time, and grew up with this mission being as much a part of our daily lives as was air and water. As an only child, with no close relatives in Tennessee, my idea of family was the church.

Although I grew up as part of the story, I was not aware of the real significance of their lives until later. About 1955 I asked my mother, Emma Risetter, to begin writing some of the stories about both my father and mother. I am grateful to her for the many pages she wrote to me. I am also grateful to others such as Grace Quinn, Letah Banks, Armethia Lively, Marie Duncan, and Robbie Wilson for sharing stories and information with me. Some of the names of the people have been changed to protect their identity.

In a few instances a footnote is included at the end of the chapter to explain a term or historical event, if the reader is interested in more details.

The story is written from my viewpoint as a child, living during the Great Depression, much as pioneers had lived for centuries. We had no electricity, running water, telephone, or car. But from this story children can learn to solve some of the same types of problems today and the need to persevere to reach a goal and to trust in God.

My prayer is that this book will help children to make the same decision that my granddaughter Way Anne did when I read her two chapters, and told her briefly the rest of the story. She was quiet for awhile, but not for long.

"Grandma, when I grow up, I'm going to be baptized too, and ask Jesus to wash my sins away."

"Yes, indeed, Way Anne. That is what you will do."

"Were my mama and daddy baptized?"

"Yes, they were. Many years ago, when they were young."

Way Anne did not know of course, that she had made Grandma's heart very happy for two reasons: first and best, because she had shown a real interest in making a commitment to Jesus herself, and second, because perhaps Grandma's book can be used by God to help other children to make the same commitment.

That is my goal and my prayer.

Ruth Risetter Watson

DEDICATION

To my children Linda, Jim, and Cindy, and my granddaughters Way Anne and Whitney, who loved to listen to my stories, and to my husband Paul and daughter Cindy who encouraged me to write these stories down in this book.

CHAPTER 1

BOAT DOWNSTAIRS

1927

In the middle of the dark night Ruth sat up in bed. A wild wind whistled and rain pounded and hammered at the windows, just like for the last two days. Now during the blackness the storm was more frightful than ever to a little girl going on four.

"Mama!" she called. "What's happening?"

Her mother came and patted her head. "It's OK. Just the rain getting worse with the strong wind blowing. We'll try to go back to sleep." But the girl lay awake a long time, listening to the raindrops fall. They sounded like pebbles pelting the roof.

The next morning she got up and stood at the window, blue eyes wide open and anxious. Her red hair looked like a wreath of gold around her head. She wore a sweater over a starched blue dress with wide scallops at the bottom. Underneath it she had on matching starched blue bloomers and black stockings. She watched streams and puddles grow in the yard and the river grow wider and wider. She turned her head to look at her father who had come to stand beside her. He was tall and slim, with the same red hair and blue eyes she had. His face was solemn and serious, with no trace of a smile.

"Daddy, the river is getting bigger! Look how muddy it is!"

"It does look scary alright. Never saw a river come up so fast."

"What's going to happen?"

"We'll be safe, no matter what the storm does to the river. If it gets higher and higher we'll just go camping in the attic! Remember what a fun place it is to play?"

Ruth often returned to the window. She watched the angry river begin to swirl over the banks, carrying sticks and leaves. The foam whirled over the grass where she played, then even over the tops of the willow bushes beside the river. She listened as the rain pounded and the river roared. She couldn't leave the window, fascinated by the fast strong water so new and strange. But as it crept up over the street in front of the house, she became alarmed.

"The river is coming after us, Daddy! Will it come inside?" Her voice trembled as if she were going to cry.

"Remember our plan? We're going to camp in the attic! Look; your mother has already started boxing up our things. We'll carry everything up the stairs and live under the roof!"

Her mother was busy packing. She had red hair too. It was long and coiled in a bun on the back of her head. She wore a long sleeved cotton dress and white apron over the top. Daddy and Ruth helped her pack everything they could in boxes or bags. They carried the things up the dark narrow stairs to the attic. Up and down they went, carrying bedding, coal oil[1] lamps, food, clothes, water, pots, dishes, books, and Daddy's black case with the violin inside. Ruth brought up her treasures: her doll Sophie in her little chair, and everything else small that she could carry. For Daddy it was especially hard. Each load seemed more of a struggle for him than the last. The muddy water crept up their front steps, then over the porch, under the front door, and began to spread over their floor as they carried up the last bundles.

"Wore me out," said Daddy as he lay down on a pile of blankets and pillows they had carried upstairs.

"Wore me out," echoed Ruth, as she plopped down beside him. "I'm scared, Daddy. Will the water get up here?"

---

1. COAL OIL. Commonly called kerosene today. Coal oil lamps and candles were once the common lighting for homes. First refined from coal by Abraham Gesner in 1854, it is now refined from the black petroleum found in the earth. Gasoline is mixed with kerosene to make diesel fuel, widely used by jet aircraft and trucks.

"No, Little Peach. Rain's stopped now. Quit raining while we were carrying our stuff up here. Aren't you glad for this attic, Emma?"

"Sure thankful for this attic," Mama said. "Ruth, you were a good girl to help us carry as many things as you could. Don't know how we could have done it without you."

Mama made pallet beds on the attic floor with the pile of blankets and quilts and pillows. Daddy opened his violin case, tuned the strings, and drew the bow across them. The violin began to sing. Soon they sang along with it, "Safe in the arms of Jesus, safe on His gentle breast." Together they repeated their favorite text: "Let not your heart be troubled: ye believe in God, believe also in Me." (John 14:1) They knelt and Mama prayed, "Dear Jesus, thank You for giving us a safe place here in the attic. Please help us to not have troubled hearts tonight." Mama turned down the wick on the coal oil lamp and blew it out.

It was terribly dark. Ruth could hear the floodwater gurgle and swish and swirl about in their house below. She wondered if her bed was covered with the muddy water. She wondered if she could ever sleep in this strange hard bed on the floor. She wondered if the water would chase her up to the attic before morning. Of course, Daddy had said they would be safe, but still she wondered . A story would help.

"Daddy, tell me a story."

"Which one, Little Peach?"

"About the blanket of sugar."

"A long time ago, when I was a little boy back in Lee, Illinois, I ran downstairs one morning and looked out the window. Something really strange had happened during the night! The fence posts wore white caps; branches on the trees were loaded with the white stuff, the ground was all covered with it! I didn't know what it could be. I remembered the sugar bowl on our table and the white sugar in it. So I called out, 'Look at the blanket of sugar!'

My mother laughed and told me, 'That's snow! You can go outside and play in it soon.'"

"And did you play in it?"

"We certainly did. We rode on a sled and flew down the hill like the wind. And we rolled up balls of it and put them on top of each other and made a snowman." And as he told stories, Ruth fell fast asleep.

The next morning they heard the water still swishing and rushing in their house below them. They peeked down the steps and saw the muddy flood was about four feet deep inside the house. They ate some bread and fruit that they had carried up the day before, and settled in to wait for the flood to go down. After a couple of hours, they heard different splashing, sloshing sounds.

"Sounds almost like somebody paddling a boat in the water. Wonder if anyone is down there."

"Hello, hello! Anybody here need help?" a booming voice called out below them. Daddy stepped cautiously as far down the attic steps as he could to peek below. There in their living room was a boat with a man in it!

"Well, I never! A boat downstairs in my house!" said Daddy. "Yes, we're OK. Finding a lot of people?"

"Yeah, lots. Flood's real bad. Covers several blocks of the town. Couple of houses washed out in the flood. Want me to take you out to the rescue station?"

"Thanks anyway. We'll stay here. Have plenty of food and water."

The boatman paddled out the front door. Through the tiny attic window, Ruth watched him float away on the lake around their house. All she could see was brown muddy water, with trees, cans, bottles, and trash, swirling crazily around in it. There was no street, no grassy river bank. It was unreal, like something out of a storybook.

Slowly the water began to go down. By evening it was only about three feet deep. They ate dry bread and canned beans and peaches again.

The next morning was the same cold food breakfast, morning worship, then nothing to do. Ruth fiddled with her toys, then stared out the attic window at the muddy

Ruth watched him float away in a sea of brown muddy water.

water below. Would the swirly mess ever become her gentle river again? Would she ever hunt pebbles and dandelions and four leaf clovers on its banks again? Would she ever live downstairs again? So much for then—what to do now? She spied Daddy's black case he carried when he sold his Bible books. She got permission to look at it, and found weird pictures she couldn't understand. Animals she had seen in her books, but nothing like these. These lions and bears and leopards had crazy heads and horns and crowns.

"Daddy, what's the matter with these animals? This leopard has four heads!"

"Those animals stand for countries and the crazy heads and horns stand for something that happened in those countries."

"Is that really in the Bible?"

"Yes, it's really in the Bible. God gave Daniel a message ahead of time of what was going to happen."

"Do people like to buy these books?"

"They are very happy to get these books. Sometimes they tell me they have been waiting many years to know things like why all these crazy animals are in the Bible. So that's why I go out every week—to give them a chance to learn about God's special messages for us today."

For two more days they waited and watched through the tiny window and peeked down the stairs. Finally the muddy river had crawled away from the house and porch. Daddy went down carefully and called back up.

"Emma, you can come on down, but tell Little Peach to wait upstairs till we get some of this mud cleaned up."

Ruth sat on the stairs and watched. Their clean little home was covered with mud, deep mud, on the floor, the furniture, and the walls. The smell was like wet garbage that had been standing for many days. She held her nose. Her parents shoveled the mud up from the floor and carried it outside in buckets. They brushed and swept and scrubbed with rags for days. After a week of cleaning and drying out, they carried everything back downstairs and put it away. The place was still damp and smelled musty and moldy. The river was its old quiet self in its proper place though its banks were slimy and smooth with mud. But they were home again and Ruth was happy to sleep in her own bed. God had kept them safe.

CHAPTER 2

HANDS IN TROUBLE

1927

After the flood and clean-up were over, Daddy dressed in his good gray suit and matching gray felt hat. He picked up his black bag.

"Have to go sell books again, Little Peach," he said. "See you Friday."

He left to again walk the roads around Pineville, Kentucky and sell his Bible books. On Friday Ruth waited for him as usual. But when she saw him, he walked as if his little black bag was much too heavy for him. His shoulders sagged and his face sagged.

"Daddy's home!" she yelled and made a dash for him. But when she met him, he didn't even seem to care that she was there.

"Welcome home, Knudt!" said Mama. He said nothing. He seemed hardly able to walk. He tossed his bag on a chair, went straight to the bedroom, and threw himself across the bed. He slept so soundly that he didn't even wake up for supper. Mama spread a blanket over him.

"Why is Daddy so tired when he comes home? He doesn't even pick me up and hold me like he used to do. Really he acts like I'm not even here."

"I really don't know, dear. Every week he seems more and more tired."

"The next morning Ruth was standing by the bed looking at her father's hands when he woke up.

"Good morning, Little Peach. Sorry I didn't say much to you last night. I was so tired. It was all I could do to get to bed." He held out his hand to her.

"That's O. K. But Daddy, what's wrong with your hands?" She began to stroke the rough and flaky skin.

7

"Don't really know. Getting old, I guess."

He picked up Ruth, and everything seemed all right again. But it was the same next week, and the next. Spring and summer passed. When Daddy came home he was always too tired to talk or eat. He never smiled and paid little attention to Ruth. The backs of his hands were burning and itching and flaking.

"I get all tuckered out so easily, Emma," he said one morning. "Another weird thing; my hands are covered with spots and burning like fire."

"I've noticed your hands. They look rough, almost as if they were covered with scales or you were shedding your skin. Are you still having trouble getting good food to eat?"

"Oh, yes. Eat mostly biscuits and cornbread. Now I hardly want to eat at all."

."Knudt, you seem so tired that you can scarcely stand. I think you should go to a doctor and find out what's wrong." So finally Daddy visited Dr. Lane.

When he came home, Ruth wanted to know what was wrong.

"Doc says I have pellagra. That's why I'm so tired, and my hands are itchy and scaly and covered with patches."

"Why?"

"Haven't been getting enough fresh garden food, like greens and carrots."

"But that's what we eat!"

"Yeah, Little Peach. Here at home. But out in the country I get very few vegetables."

"Will you ever get well?"

"Oh, yes. We'll plant our own garden and grow our own fruit and vegetables and eat lots of them."

"Where are we going to plant the garden?" asked Ruth.

"No place here in town. Got to find a farm somewhere."

A few days after Daddy talked about planting a garden, someone knocked. Daddy went to the door, and there stood a big burly man.

"Come in, Brother Hickman! We've been looking for you!"

Ruth was afraid of the enormous man. He had wide shoulders. His hair and eyebrows and mustache were black and thick. He wore suspenders hooked over his huge belly. She quickly hid under the table. Mama said, "It's alright. This is Brother Hickman. He's Daddy's boss." But Ruth wouldn't budge out of her hiding place. She could hear the important talk just as well there.

"How's the book work going, Brother Risetter?" he began.

"The book work is going great. I find many people who want to buy these good books, if I have the strength to get to them. But I have a big problem. I have pellegra. I am tired most of the time, and by the weekend I am so worn out that when I come home I can't even think of eating. Don't even want to talk. I just want to sleep. It makes my hands rough and scaly and burn and itch. I don't see how I can keep working."

"So that's why you sent for me?"

"Exactly."

"Did the doctor tell you what caused the pellagra?"

"Not enough vitamins. I can't get good vegetarian food out in the country where I've been working. Everybody cooks with pork and even the vegetables are swimming in pig grease. There's very little I can eat. Now I'm sick—too sick to keep on working and eating."

Brother Hickman's forehead wrinkled up and his face clouded over. "I remember you told me four years ago when you came to Kentucky to work that you wanted to start a church here by selling books. So I know you don't want to stop."

"That's been my dream. But it is impossible for me to go like this. It is such a disappointment for me, for I haven't started any church. What can I do?"

"Brother Risetter, we like having you and your family work here in Kentucky to sell books. But the time has come to stop. You must move to a farm and grow plenty of fruit and vegetables to eat so you can get well. Any way you could buy yourself a farm?"

"Well, I have a little money left from my inheritance. Not enough to buy a farm here in Kentucky, though. You have any ideas?"

"I'm moving my family south to Collegedale, Tennessee, near Southern Junior College, so my children can go to school there. Farms are a lot less expensive down there. Why don't you come to Tennessee too? You can start a church there. You could even sell books again when you get well."

"Good idea. Perhaps that is what we should do."

Mr. Hickman stood up, then leaned over and peeked under the table. He looked straight at Ruth and said, "Don't be afraid. Your daddy will get strong again. Maybe you can live on a farm and have a kitten and baby chicks. Would you like that?"

Ruth nodded solemnly at the big man but could not say one word. He did not seem quite so frightening now.

After he left, Daddy explained it all to Ruth. "We're going to move to Tennessee to find our farm!"

Daddy was so pleased and excited about it all that it rubbed off on Ruth too.

"And we'll have kittens and baby chickens?"

"Probably lots of them!"

"But—how will we find our farm?"

"We have a Friend there already to help us."

"Really?"

"Yes, really—the same Friend who helped us camp safely in the attic when the flood came. God will help us find the right farm." He reached down and patted the little redhead beside him. She looked up at Daddy and Mama. Everything would be OK now. She had wished for a sister. Now she would have real live playmates—baby chicks and kittens.

A few days later Daddy drove home a shiny black Model T Ford.[1] "Come go for a ride with me in the tin Lizzie!"

He had left the engine running. They all piled into beautiful Lizzie and Daddy took them around the block. It had a long seat across the front, and a closed in back. "Look at all the space! We can carry all our stuff to Tennessee in it. Later we can use it to carry people to church!"

This move was much bigger and harder than the one up into the attic to get away from the flood. They began packing boxes with dishes and books and clothes. Ruth packed Sophie with her chair and the other toys. They stacked Lizzie full of boxes and trunks and the walnut bookcase with glass doors. Finally they finished and were ready to go. The little house was empty now.

It was early morning with just enough dawn to see the house standing there left alone. The October air was quiet and cold. Mama and Ruth climbed up the running board and scooted down the padded seat.

"Don't be scared when I crank Lizzie," said Daddy.

"Do be careful," said Mama. "You know many men have broken their arms or sprained their wrists cranking."

"I'll be careful. Just sit tight and don't scream or jump out."

He reached over the wheel and set two levers. Then he jumped down and walked to the front of the hood. He grabbed the crank with his right hand, and slipped his left forefinger through a loop of wire to control the choke. He pulled the wire loop and turned the crank lever with a quick strong pull. Nothing happened. He did it again.

---

1   Model T's were made by Henry Ford from 1908–1927. In 1896 Ford made his first horseless carriage, guided with a stick. Most people thought it was like a roller coaster: lots of fun, but why buy one for themselves? Ford made them at such a low price many people could afford them and by 1927 fifteen million or more than half of all the cars on the road were Model T's, commonly called Tin Lizzie or flivver. Ford's next car was the Model A. Many other companies tried to make cars too but they failed. Between 1900 and 1938 more than one thousand companies tried to make cars and went out of business.

The morning quiet split wide open with the roaring noise. The car jolted awake and jerked like it was having a coughing fit.

Daddy jumped back on the running board and landed safe inside. He grabbed the steering wheel.

"Whew! Knudt, I wish you'd bought the one with a self starter."

"Been easier alright, but the self starter costs more. Lizzie cost $600 as it was."

Daddy drove and drove until all the houses of Pineville were gone and there was only the road, bordered by trees dressed in fiery red, gold, bronze, and yellow with evergreens sprinkled among them. Some of the trees were already bare because the leaves had fallen off. The sky was like a great bowl above them, that always traveled along wherever they went. Beyond the trees were hills on either side of the road. The hills looked like they were painted with the same colors as the trees next to the road.

By the time the sun was high overhead they saw a sign beside the road.

"Guess what! We are in Tennessee!" said Mama

"Really? This is Tennessee? It doesn't look any different."

"You're right. Looks very much the same."

After a stop for a lunch picnic they piled into the car again and drove and drove. Ruth began to get tired of looking at trees and hills.

"Tell me about the kittens and baby chicks we'll have on our farm, Mama," she asked. "Did you have baby chicks when you were a little girl?"

"Oh, yes, we had baby chicks—but only in the spring. We had red hens called Rhode Island Reds. When they wanted to hatch baby chicks, they would spread out their wings and pretend to be covering little chicks. Then we knew they wanted to hatch eggs, so we would give them a nest full of eggs and they would sit on them for three weeks. The baby chicks would peck their way out of the shells and could run around as soon as they hatched out."

"Could you hold them?"

"Yes, you could hold them—but very gently."

Daddy said, "When I was a little boy I was so happy to see the baby chicks that I picked one up and held it so tightly that I squeezed it to death. I was heart broken when I saw the squashed lump of yellow feathers in my hand. So you can't squeeze them like Sophie!"

The sun began to drop lower and lower and the edge of the sky turned pink. Ruth watched the houses cluster closer and closer together along the highway.

"Knoxville! Here we are! Now let's find a place to sleep tonight."

Mama and Daddy began reading the signs. One said, "Tourist Home". They parked Lizzie and Daddy went inside.

He came back and said, "Great place, kind owner, $2.00 a night for all of us and we get breakfast too. We'll stay here." They took out the suitcases they would need for the night. It was a really great place. There was a white picket fence all around and a white gatepost on either side of the picket gate. It looked safe. But Ruth had no idea how such a simple post could hold such a fright for her, and soon.

CHAPTER 3

FINDING BIG SISTER

1927

Day after day Ruth and her family looked for farms for sale around Knoxville, Tennessee. Day after day they talked to strange people and in the evenings they drove back to the Tourist Home to their cozy beds. But one night the Tourist Home had changed.

Out of the night blackness, a fiery monster on a post glared down at Ruth. Strange lighted holes made it look like a face on fire. The girl hung close to her mama's skirts. This fright was different from the flood that had crawled out of the river and into their house a few months ago but a fright just the same. To get inside they had to pass the gatepost where the fiery monster perched.

"It's only a pumpkin," her father said. "Somebody cut out those holes for eyes, nose, and mouth, and put a lighted candle inside. It's called a jack-o-lantern, made just for fun for Halloween. Come with me, and we'll touch it. Feel the outside of the shell, like this."

She fearfully touched it with one finger. Truly it was just a pumpkin.

"That's not fun. It's scary." And it was harder than ever to go to sleep that night in her strange bed.

The next morning the family drove downtown and stopped at Mr. Michler's real estate office again where they had gone day after day to find farms for sale.

"Find your farm yesterday?" Mr. Michler asked.

"Not yet. Have any others?"

"Have a very isolated place, 40 miles from Knoxville. Owners want to move to Florida. It's on a narrow dirt

road way back in "hill billy" country, where bootleggers[1]
have a law of their own. "

"What do you mean, a law of their own?"

"Those people make their own liquor. They hide away
in places they dig out on the mountains, called stills. The
government can't do much about stopping them. It's wild
and woolly country. You're pretty much on your own."

"Let's see it. Bootleggers won't be a problem, because
I never use their liquor. Give us directions, please."

Soon the family headed out of Knoxville for 40 miles
of road that twisted and turned. For a long time Ruth was
very quiet. Finally she said, "Daddy, what is liquor?"

"It's a drink that makes people act silly and stupid
and stagger around. People called bootleggers hide away
in the hills and make it from corn. They sell it or drink
it themselves. Sometimes they call it moonshine because
they make it at night in the dark."

After a couple of hours they found Oliver Springs.
It was a village of a few stores, with false fronts making them look tall, a post office, a bank, a train station,
churches, and a cluster of houses. They took a dirt road
into narrow Hen Valley. There was just room between
the hills for the road, the railroad, and small fields of
brown dry cornstalks. After about four miles they saw a
weathered gray clapboard house, cradled in shrubs and
wisteria arbors. Behind it stood Walden's Ridge, with a
blanket of gold and green trees flung over it.

Daddy parked in the yard. Three people came outside
to meet them. Visitors were clearly a great event, especially in a car. The man looked kind of faded, with his
worn overalls, wrinkles, and gray hair. So did the woman,
with her flour sack dress and apron. But the girl looked
crisp and new, with clear bright hair and skin. Her eyes

---

1   Bootlegger. One who made and sold alcohol illegally.
January 16, 1920, the 18th Amendment to the Constitution
went into effect, which made it illegal to produce liquor.
Bootleggers got rich making liquor in homemade stills across
the country. Between 1921 and 1925, almost 700,000 stills
were seized by the government. In most cities a person in
could find liquor in anywhere from three to thirty minutes.
By 1929 it was impossible to enforce the Prohibition
Amendment. It was repealed in December, 1933.

sparkled, too. Although she was tall like the grownups, she stood up straight, not stooped like they did. Somehow her flour sack dress seemed fresher and prettier. She smiled shyly at Ruth. Ruth smiled back, then quickly hid behind her mama's skirts.

"Hello! You must be the Blankenbucklers. I am Knudt Risetter, and this is my wife and daughter. Mr. Michler sent us. He said you want to sell your place."

Mr. Blankenbuckler said, "Pleased to meet cha. This is my wife and my daughter Ophelia. Yep, we shore do want to sell the place. You all come on in and set a spell. Where you'uns be from?"

Everybody sat down in the cane seated chairs around the fireplace.

"Just moving down from Kentucky. I grew up on a farm in Illinois."

"So you all are aiming to get back on the farm again. Well, it's getting harder and harder for me to keep up with all the work. The winter's bad on my arthritis too. So I'm going to Florida. I hear tell it never gets cold down there."

The grown men talked some more. Finally the man said,

"I'd be right pleasured to show you all what we've got. We've got two pieces, 111 acres altogether. Goes half way up this here mountain, called Walden's Ridge. It's got a barn, a shed for your tools and split wood. I'll give you the two horses, two cows, a calf, and chickens. The loft's plumb full of new hay for winter, and the barn shed's done got everything you'll need for farming: plows, mower, hayrake, harrow, disc, wagon, and buggy. There's a crik just below the barn to water the stock, and it never runs dry. The well's right handy to the kitchen door, and it's got sweet spring water."

Ruth and the Blankenbuckler's daughter eyed each other up and down while all the talk was going on.

Daddy said, "Let's go see it." So the men went out to walk over the place.

Mrs. Blankenbuckler began to take Mama around the house.

"Ophelia, why don't you take this young'un around and show her the chickens."

So Ophelia asked Ruth, "Want to see the chickens? You can feed them if you want to." Ruth nodded, and silently followed the older girl outside.

Ophelia yelled out, "Chick-eee, chick-eee, chick-eee!" Fat red hens ran and flew to her and crowded around excitedly squawking, "Cawk, cawk, cawk." Ruth pulled her skirt tight about her. She wasn't sure about all these feathered creatures so close.

"I'll show you. Take some corn in your hand, and throw it out on the ground, like this." The flock gobbled up every kernel. Ruth tried it too and squealed when the hens ate her corn. Ophelia squatted down to chicken height, and held out corn in her hand. The hens snapped it up quickly.

"You can do it. Feed them in your hand, like this." Ruth did, and laughed out loud as the sharp little beaks gobbled up her corn too.

"They ate it!" This was a new game she had never played before.

"But where are the baby chicks?"

"Have to wait till spring for them. They'd freeze to death in the winter."

So Ruth would have to wait awhile for the baby chicks. But never mind, Ophelia was better than any baby chicks could possibly be. Now Ruth was eager to follow Ophelia wherever she went.

"I'll show you my room." She led Ruth inside and up very steep stairs to the second floor. The first room was very dark, with unfinished walls and no ceiling, and only the tin roof for a covering. Then she led Ruth into another room which had been finished with unplaned boards. The walls were rough and splintery.

"This is where I sleep," said Ophelia. "I can hear the katydids real good up here so close to the treetops. Here's another room, just like mine."

Then a horrible hissing, chugging noise filled the house. It rattled the windows and stopped all talk. Ruth stood aside and her eyes clung to Ophelia.

"Are you scared?"

Ruth nodded, unable to speak.

"It's just the train. You'll get used to it."

After awhile, Ophelia said, "I gotta go outdoors." Of course Ruth followed her.

This time she took the path behind the house past the grape arbor. They came to the outhouse, hidden behind a giant clump of pampas grass.

"You can come in too. Hit's got two seats." Sure enough, this spacious outhouse had holes for two people. So there would be no need to worry if you had to go and somebody else was already using one hole. There was plenty of paper handy too—the Sears Roebuck catalog. But they wouldn't stay long. The outhouse was built over a huge pit. People had used that toilet for years -- thousands of times. The rotting stench rose up into their noses and almost made Ruth sick. In sympathy, Ophelia held her nose.

"Phew! It sure stinks all right. But you'll get used to it."

Next they petted Tom, the great yellow cat. Ruth looked for the kittens. Perhaps she would have to wait for spring for kittens too. They looked for eggs in the boxes lined with hay in the barn shed.

"The make-believe egg in the box is to give the hens the idea that is a good place to lay their eggs," said Ophelia. "But sometimes they want to make their own nests in the bushes anyhow. So let's go look for their hidden nests." They found six more eggs in the bushes. By now Ruth knew Ophelia was wonderful. Ruth had no brothers or sisters. But now she had a new big sister to show her such fun things to see and do. The younger girl followed the teen-ager like a puppy. Ophelia had made this farm like home already—complete with a sister.

After some time the girls saw the men come back to the house, and followed them inside. Daddy had seen the barn stocked full of hay for the horses and cows, plows to turn the soil, and haying implements. He had seen the garden space, the grape arbor, toolshed, woodshed, well with shed, apple trees, and woods. It was home.

Mama had seen the rustic beauty of the weathered farmhouse, the potted flowers, the shrubs cradling the house and promising bright forsythia, bridal wreath, japonica and snowballs in the spring, and the cellar stocked with jars of food already canned for the winter. It was home.

Ruth had found her wonderful "big sister," Ophelia. It was home.

Everybody gathered in the front room, sitting in straight ladder backed chairs around the fireplace. The glowing coals warmed their chilly hands. The grownups talked very solemnly about grown-up things such as crops, garden, hay and potatoes ready for the winter, the price, and such. Then the faded farmer's face clouded over. He began to talk very slowly, choosing his words carefully.

"I gotta warn you. The neighbor across the road—Ed Russell—he's one to stay clear of. He's gotta have his likker—whether he bootlegs it himself, or gets it off some body else. Just don't cross him. Another one you don't cross with is Hank Scarborough."

"No problem. I don't drink, so I'll never have any business with him."

"O. K. Just wanted you to know. One more thing, a little request. Our big yellow cat. Would you give Old Tom a home till he dies?" His voice was very low, and he drew one hand across his eyes, as if he had a bug or something to clean away.

Daddy said, "You can count on it. We'll take good care of Old Tom. Your place looks good. I think we can grow what we need here. My wife likes all the flowers and shrubs. She's a great flower lover. What do you say, Ruth? Think you would like to play here?"

Ruth looked up at Ophelia, and nodded. They grinned at each other. Ophelia reached out and squeezed Ruth's hand.

"Then it's settled. Where do we go to sign the papers?"

"We'll go to Kingston tomorrow and get the deed in your name."

So on November 1, 1927, the grown folks drove to Kingston and officially bought the place. Ruth stayed with her new "big sister," Ophelia.

For two weeks after the papers were signed, the Blankenbucklers were busy packing up. They invited the Ri-

"You got to drop it fast, lickety split, else it won't get any water."

setters to move into their front bedroom, which had its own fireplace to keep them warm on the chilly November days.

Every minute that Ophelia could spare from helping with the packing she showed Ruth new wonders of the farm. They climbed up to the barn loft and jumped up and down in the sweet hay. They sat on it, and chewed on the fresh dry stalks together.

At the well house just outside the back porch, Ophelia said, "Let me teach you how to get a drink of fresh water." She unwound the handle fast so the rope would drop the bucket quickly into the water below.

"You got to drop it fast, lickety split, else it won't get any water. If you let it down gentle like, it'll just float and won't ever fill. Sometimes you can pull it up a little and drop it again, fill it a little more, then drop it again and again till it's full." She pulled up the bucket, lifted a shiny tin dipper from a hook on the well house, and gave Ruth a dipper full of the fresh water. It tasted good.

"I want to tell you about Marie Russell. She lives in that log cabin across the railroad and road. She comes over to get water because they don't have a well. You'll like her. She's very nice but her dad is a terror." Later, just as Ophelia had said, Marie brought her bucket to get water.

"This is Marie," said Ophelia. "Marie, maybe you can help this young-un get used to the farm—later."

Another day they crept down the dark steps into the cellar, damp and musty with rows of potted plants, and shelves of glass jars filled with canned beans, sauerkraut, tomatoes, apples, and peaches. The plants and food stored there would be safe from freezing. They petted the horses, the cows, and Old Tom. They smelled the fragrant herbs hanging on the back porch to dry: sage, dill, horseradish, and such. Ophelia showed Ruth where the gooseberry bushes were, where rhubarb would come up next spring and where the beechnut tree stood down by the creek, with its naked roots, just right to play on. Wonderful Ophelia. Ruth loved Ophelia.

After two weeks, the Blankenbucklers had finished packing and were ready to go to sunny Florida. Neighbors gathered round for their last words. Ophelia's brother Bob, who lived just a mile away down the railroad tracks, came to go with his folks to the train. They piled their boxes and barrels in Daddy's tin Lizzie. He was to take them to Oliver Springs to the train station.

"Remember, my son Bob here, he'll help you with anything you need." Everybody was weepy and sad. Ruth stood by, holding tight to Ophelia's hand. When everybody was packed in, the most terrible thing happened! Ophelia reached down and gave Ruth a big hug.

"My big brother Bob will take good care of you, Ruth. Remember me when you hunt for eggs—and eat gooseberry pies next summer!" And Ophelia got into the Ford and left with her parents! How terrible! Somehow Ruth had had no idea that Ophelia would move away with her folks! How she cried and cried to lose her wonderful new big sister.

That night they sat by the fireplace. Ruth was sad about losing Ophelia. Daddy gathered her up in his arms, wrapped a blanket around her and held her close in the big rocking chair.

"Little Peach, I know you're sad to lose Ophelia. But you will be happy here. There won't be any floods or jack-o-lanterns to scare you. We're safe—at home."

Mama was happy too. "Finally, a home of our own. God is good. This is the perfect place for you, Knudt, to get plenty of vegetables and cure this pellagra. I just wish Ed Russell didn't live so close. Sure hope he and Hank Scarborough don't cause us any trouble."

"No fear, Emma. I'm sure the government will take care of them."

"Daddy, what's government?"

"It's the big boss over everybody. People vote to choose officials of government. Then these officials make rules, collect taxes, take a census, build roads, put robbers in jail, and such work."

"What's a census?"

"A census is counting everybody in the whole country."

"Well, Daddy, we don't need any government. We already have a road, and a house of our own, and I sure won't let them count me."

Daddy smiled, and began singing softly,

"Home, home, sweet, sweet home,
Be it ever so humble, there's no place like home."

Ruth did not hear the rest of the song, nor the evening prayer. She was home, safe at last, even if she had lost her new big sister. But she would never forget Ophelia.

CHAPTER 4

FRIENDS AND NEIGHBORS

1927

Ruth stirred in her sleep. Was it morning? She seemed to hear snapping and popping. Was she dreaming? No. She remembered. She was home, in her bed, right next to the door into the living room. Her parents' big bed was in the farthest corner of the bedroom, and she had the corner closest to the warm living room. She slid out of bed and softly pattered into the living room. There in the fireplace golden flames danced above hickory logs, from time to time shooting streams of sparks upward as they made the crackling noises she had heard. She stood close to soak up the warmness.

"Come out into the kitchen," Mama called. "I made a hot fire in the stove, and it's cozy here too. Soon Daddy will be coming in with the milk."

Ruth had to run through the cold dining room to get to the kitchen which was warm too. Corn dodgers were baking in the oven. Beans were boiling in a black iron pot on top of the cookstove. There were four holes with black lids on top of the black stove; two were over the oven and two were directly over the firebox where the fire burned. The silvery lid handle stood up from one lid, with its narrow hooked end fastened under a tiny bar across a cut out depression on the lid itself. Mama had taken off the lid from one of the holes, and set the bean pot directly over the hot fire to cook faster. Now Mama lifted the pot of beans out of the hole over the fire, and set it on the back of the stove. The she lifted the black lid with the silvery handle, and set the lid back in its hole directly over the fire.

Daddy came in with two buckets full of milk, and white froth bubbling so high it looked like soap bubbles on top.

"Those cows are good milkers. Let their milk down easy. I've got about two gallons of milk for us." He went to the washstand to clean up. He dipped the shiny long handled dipper into the white enamel bucket of water on the washstand, and poured two dippers full of water into the wash basin. He washed his hands with the water and the bar of brown Octagon soap on the stand. Then he opened the kitchen door and threw his used water outside. He dried his hands on the flour sack hanging from a nail on the wall.

"Then we'll have plenty of milk to drink," said Mama. "We can make butter and sour cream and cottage cheese too. You'll be well in no time, Knudt, certainly in the spring when we get the garden growing." Mama laid a cheesecloth over the top of one bucket, and twisted it tightly with one hand. With the other hand she grasped the bucket, and poured the milk through the cloth into a white crock on the table. When she took off the cheesecloth, Ruth saw tiny specks of hay and dirt on the cheesecloth, that had been strained out of the milk. After she did the same with the other bucket, she covered the crocks with clean flour sacks and set them on a shelf on the porch to cool. The family gathered around the table, and Daddy prayed, "Dear God, thank You for this peaceful place with plenty of food and fresh air. Grant us Your blessing on this food. Amen."

They sat close to the warm stove to eat their crisp corn dodgers with the beans and milk.

Daddy said, "Emma, it's comfortable here in the kitchen, and in the living room. But that dining room between the kitchen and the living room is cold. What would you think if we took out the dining room fireplace, closed up the fireplace hole, and moved this kitchen stove into the dining room for the winter? We could move it back here in the spring."

"Wonderful idea. That would keep the dining room warmer."

"Let's do it. First we must tear out the hearth in the dining room, and put in that new floor I promised you. That dining room floor looks like we could fall through it any day. We'll go to Oliver Springs[1] today to get materials."

Shortly the family piled into the new Model T and set off for town. The air was crisp and cold. Pockets of white frost lay hidden in shadows that the sunshine had not yet reached. Blue smoke curled upward from the chimney of each cabin. Here and there a cow or two huddled as closely as possible to a sheltering haystack in a field. Nobody was stirring; fields were empty except for a few shocks of dry brown cornstalks. They met no other car, not even a horse. They bumped about as they hit holes and washouts in the hard clay road.

Just before they reached Oliver Springs, Ruth spotted a dazzling creature inside a fenced in yard close to the road. It looked like a huge bird, brilliant blue and green, and had large yellow eyes on its enormous tail, so long it dragged on the ground.

"Look! What's that?"

"Well, I never!" said Mama. "A peacock—out here in the mountains. You see them once in awhile in a zoo—but out here! Look at that house! Is this a palace? Makes me think of the mansions wealthy people have in Los Angeles and Minneapolis."

---

1 Oliver Springs. Built at the site of nine mineral springs which deposited colored minerals as they overflowed—red, purple, lavender, green, and black. A grand hotel opened there in 1895 with 200 rooms, filled all the time during season. It was four stories high with a 60-foot tower on top. The Richards brothers, the owners, brought in an Italian orchestra to play for dances. When they opened the hotel, they brought in one whole box-car load of wine as a starter. There were bridle paths all over the top of Walden Ridge above the hotel. There was a billiard room, electric elevators, wine cellars, a dance pavilion, electric power plant, water and sewage systems, parlors, reading rooms, dining hall, billiard room, stage and dressing rooms, bowling alley, tennis courts, and croquet grounds. The advertising brochure claimed the mineral spring water would cure or greatly benefit stomatitis glassitis, tonsillitis, gastric ulcer, diarrhea, constipation, jaundice, cirrhosis or drunkard's liver, diseases of the urinary system, epilepsy, migraine, diseases of the blood and skin, etc.

"Somebody important must live in such a house!" said Daddy.

They crossed the railroad tracks, passed the train depot and post office, and parked in front of Sienknecht's General Store. Inside, Ruth stared and stared. On the right were men's hats, shirts, ties, underwear, socks and suits and boxes of shoes. On the left were ladies dresses, laces, ribbons, and shelves of piece goods. In the center of the store a few men sat close to the round black pot bellied stove to warm themselves, and spit their brown tobacco juice in the dirty spittoon on the floor beside the stove. A heavy sweet dusty smell from all the tobacco and leather and sacks hung in the air.

She saw sacks printed in brightly colored flowers.

Beyond the stove Ruth saw the wall covered with shiny new tools and harness fixings: hammers, short saws, crosscut saws, hoes, rakes, axes, picks, shovels, pitchforks, post hole diggers, plowshares, leather reins, horseshoes and such. Barrels of nails stood on the floor. Beyond was the grocery department. She saw barrels of loose sour pickles, crackers, flour, beans, meal, and even peanut butter.

Shelves were filled with cans of baking powder, coffee, tea, and tobacco. She could tell what the cans were by the pictures on the front. There were twisted brown leaves hanging from the ceiling.

"What are the leaves for?" Ruth asked her mother.

"Those are tobacco twists to chew. The tobacco in the cans is to roll for cigarettes and dip for snuff," said Mama.

She saw a pile of burlap sacks full of grain and cattle feed and cotton print sacks of cornmeal and flour. Some were printed in brightly colored flowers.

Daddy found the flooring he wanted, and also bought nails, chicken feed, coal oil for the lamps, a broom, cornmeal, flour, a sack of wheat, and two sheets of tin for fireplace covers. He asked the clerk about the white mansion they had passed as they came into town.

"Oh, that's the Harvey Hannah house[2]," the clerk explained. "He's our State Railroad Commissioner. Almost got to be governor 5 years ago. Grand place, ain't it, with the peacocks and marble columns and all. Oliver Springs used to be a grand place itself, before the fire. We had us a resort hotel. It was plumb fancy. Folks came from Knoxville and all over by train and in fancy carriages and fancy outfits, to bathe in the hot sulfur springs. Burned to the ground about 22 years ago, and nobody ever tried to build it back. Town hain't never been as grand since."

---

2   Harvey Hannah House. Built by state Railroad Commissioner Harvey Hannah in 1890. He was a colonel in the Spanish American War. Home has been used as a residence since them; in 2000 it was converted into a bed and breakfast. Highway built through Hen Valley in the thirties was named Harvey Hannah Highway in his honor.

As they left town, they looked more closely at the Harvey Hannah mansion.

Indeed it was a grand place, fit for a king. It was two stories high, all white, with grass that was green even this late in the year. The lawn was trimmed evenly and looked like a smooth carpet. Four sparkling white columns reached all the way up to the porch roof.

Matching windows were on each side of the wide carved door, and a bay window stuck out from the south wall. Lacy white curtains hung at all the windows. Round boxwood bushes lined the walk and the road. Ruth watched for the peacocks, and sure enough, she saw two of the regal birds walking about. The male lifted his

"Somebody important must live in that house!"

shiny green tail, so that it stood up behind him like a brilliant set of rainbows, and spread it in a great circle so that each feather showed its yellow eyespot ringed with bronze. Its great tail shimmered and shook and made a rustling sound. The male had a tuft on its head. The mate was plain, with no train and head ornament.

The next day, Daddy began to lay the new floor in the dining room. First he tore out the fireplace and hearth and covered the chimney hole with a sheet of tin he had bought at Schnicknicks. He made a small hole high in the chimney just big enough for the stovepipe. Next he began to tear out the rough and rotten flooring, and soon Ruth could see long beams underneath, lined up from wall to wall. Daddy told her these were joists.

Ruth rubbed her finger on the satiny new boards from Oliver Springs. Each board had a ridge running along the side all the way to both ends. On the other side, it had a groove cut into the board so the next ridge would fit neatly into it. This floor would be smooth and tight. After Daddy had torn out all the old boards, he took a piece of the new flooring and pushed it as close to the wall as he could. Ruth handed him nails from the paper sack, and he hammered those nails down so the floor was tightly fastened to the joists. Then he fit another board into the first and nailed it down the same way.

"Howdy!" called somebody outside. Daddy went out to greet their visitor. Ruth followed close behind.

"Howdy. Jus' thought I'd come by and see how my new neighbors a doing. Name's Ed Russell."

"Hello. Glad to have a neighbor drop by. My name's Risetter, Knudt Risetter, that is. Won't you come inside and get warm? We're in a bit of a mess just now, putting in a new floor in the dining room."

"Nope, I'll not come in this time. Jus' wanted to meet you. Where you all from? Never heerd of the name Rister in these here parts."

"We just moved down from Kentucky."

Ruth clung close to Daddy as she peered around at the stranger. His overalls hung loosely on his thin body.

All his clothes and denim cap were patched and dirty, as if they had not been washed for a long long time. Sharp beady eyes glared out from between two shocks of unruly black hair, one shock sticking out from under his cap and the other growing on his chin. His smell reminded Ruth of the barnyard, and his hair reminded her of a picture she had seen once of a grizzly bear standing up to protect her cub.

"Well, let me tell you. You better have a pile of money stashed away to get along here in Hen Valley. 'Taint no trees here that grows money on 'em." Ed Russell turned his head to spit his tobacco juice out of the way on the grass. He kept looking at the shiny new Ford and the pile of new flooring. He took a plug of brown tobacco leaves out of his pocket, and offered some to Daddy.

"Thanks, Mr. Russell, I don't chew tobacco."

"Well, I couldn't get along without my 'bakker and swig of likker once in awhile."

"What do most people do here for a living?"

"Grow a little corn for the mule and likker, little 'bakker, few spuds and beans and such. Lucky ones get a job on the railroad or in the mines at Windrock.[3] If you need likker, I might could get some fer you."

"Thanks anyway, but I don't drink."

"Not ever?"

"Not ever at all."

"Well, now. How you gonna pleasure yourself these cold days if you never use 'bakker or likker? How come you don't use them?"

"Mr. Russell, you might think I'm queer, but there are some things a lot of people use that I can't, such as tobacco or liquor. It's very important for me."

---

3   Windrock Mountain mines. Opened in 1903. Oldest continuously operated mine in Tennessee, with 1,200 miles of entries and airways. At its peak 700 people lived in 170 houses in two camps. 350 men worked in the mine in 1927. A tramway car carried passengers and goods up the one mile incline and brought down the mined coal. The tunnel mines were worked until 1947 when strip mining operations layered the mountain into wide terraces where machines extracted the seams of coal. In 1983 these machines produced 8,000 tons a week with 70 men working. (Synder Roberts, The Story of Oliver Springs, Tennessee 3 volumes)

"Oh, yeah? How come?"

"You really want to know?"

"Yeah. Tell me."

"Tobacco and liquor are not good for a man's body. I have a book that tells me I shouldn't do anything to my body that ruins it."

"What kind of doctor book is that?"

"It's called the Bible. So you might say it's a religious reason. I could read it for you if you like to hear it."

"Naw, that's OK. I'll just take your word for it. I'd be a sight though if I didn't have my 'bakker and likker to take my mind offen my troubles." He paused a moment.

"We'uns live in the cabin across the road and railroad. We'd like to get us a bucket of water from your well once in a while, like we used to do from Blankenbucklers. Hain't got no well at our cabin."

"Sure, that will be fine."

"Gotta be goin'. You all come over and set a spell."

"Thanks. You all come back and see us."

Mama had heard everything, through the partly open door. "Sounds to me like he came not just to be neighborly, but to find out if we have any money."

"Seemed that way to me too.'"

"He didn't care much for your seed you tried to plant."

"No, but at least he found out that he can't sell any moonshine at this house."

"That may not make him very happy either. He would like to get new customers. Folks here think we're strange. Don't use liquor or tobacco, have an unusual name, drive a car. I haven't seen another car on this road since we've been here. I haven't seen a car parked at any of these cabins."

Ruth asked, "Mama, you said he didn't care for your seed you were trying to plant. I didn't see any seeds. What were you talking about?"

"Let me tell you a story. Once upon a time, a long time ago, a man lived that everybody called Johnny Appleseed[4]. Probably one day when he was enjoying the sweetness of a juicy apple, he thought about his old neighbors who had moved away to the wilderness along the Ohio River. They had taken wagons, tools, pots, and such things to start building their new pioneer homes. He wondered how many of them had thought to bring apple seeds. Such a little thing—a tiny hard black seed. But it would grow into a tree and give hundreds of apples to somebody—if it were planted. He had an idea. He saved the seeds from his apple, and his next apple, and the next. He began asking other people to save apple seeds too. Then one day when he had a cloth bag full of apple seeds, he set off to the Ohio River frontier himself. As he met the settlers, he gave them apple seeds, and sometimes herbs, and even religious ideas too. Of course it took years and years for the seeds to get big enough to grow apples, but they did, and many many people ate sweet juice apples later. The pioneer people thought of him almost as a prophet from the Bible days, wandering around in the wilderness, with his wonderful seeds and ideas, and they called him Johnny Appleseed."

"But—what does Johnny Appleseed have to do with Mr. Russell? I didn't see Daddy give Mr. Russell any apple seeds."

"No, no. Just wait. You see, a long time ago when your father and I first met back in Minneapolis, Minnesota, we were so happy because we both love Jesus that we decided to be like Johnny Appleseed and plant seeds. Except the seeds we want to plant are idea seeds instead of apple seeds. Whenever we can, we try to plant an idea in somebody's mind that will help that somebody think about how much Jesus loves them. We call them joy seeds. The plan is our special family secret. Planting joy seeds for Jesus. It may take a long time for them to grow up, like Johnny's apple seeds, but we keep on planting."

---

4   Johnny Appleseed became a frontier legend because he gave apple seeds to many pioneers along the Ohio River. His real name was John Chapman. He lived from 1774 to 1847.

"So when Daddy sold Bible books he was planting joy seeds?"

"Exactly! You've got the idea!"

"I wish I could plant seeds for Jesus."

"You can! For sure!"

"How?"

"First of all you have to grow the seeds and have them ready to plant."

"How do I do that?"

"By learning more memory verses, just like you learned 'Let not your heart be troubled.' Then some day you'll have a chance to plant your own joy seeds!"

"O. K. I'll work hard on growing my own seeds."

After a few days Daddy and Ruth finished laying the new floor. Stove moving day was next. They ate a cold breakfast for Mama could not start the cooking fire that morning. The stove must be cold when they moved it. She cleaned out the ashes from the box below the grate. Daddy unfastened the black stovepipe from the range, then from the chimney. The stovepipe came apart in four pieces. He took the pipes outside and poked through them with a rag tied to a stick to clean out the soot. Next Daddy held one side of the range, and Mama the other, and they pushed and dragged that heavy stove into the dining room. Daddy put the pipes back into the cookstove and then up into the chimney. Last he covered the hole in the old kitchen side of the chimney where the stove had been. He closed the door between the dining room and the kitchen. Mama started a fire in the stove, and soon the new kitchen was warm and cozy.

After the stove moving day, Marie came over to get a bucket of water, and dropped in to see Ruth.

Mama said, "Come in, child. "

"I heard about your new floor. Hit's purty! Shore feels mighty nice in here by this good fire."

"Is your place cold, Marie?" asked Ruth.

"My mama pastes newspapers on the inside of the logs. It helps, but the wind still comes in and shivers us."

The girl wore no shoes, socks, sweater, or coat, and her thin old dress did little to protect her from the icy wind.

Ruth led her new friend to her best seat, the second stair. The tall steps were hard for short legs to climb, but perfect for sitting beside the window. A Sears Roebuck catalog lay on the next stair.

"Do you think your ma would let us cut out some paper dolls from that catalog?"asked Marie.

"Sure, that's fine, no need to ask. Here is a pair of scissors."

Marie showed Ruth how to look in the catalog for pictures of girls that were standing quite straight and cut them out. Then they found other pictures of dresses that would fit over the paper dolls.

"Now you cut out the new dress, but you leave a tab on each shoulder and one on each side." After they had cut out the new dress, Marie showed Ruth how to fasten the tabs over the girl doll.

"I hear some people really do have lots of dresses, like our paper dolls. Shore be nice, wouldn't it?"

A freight train whistled "Hoot, hoot!" and roared by on the tracks, making all talk impossible. The thundering noise seemed to make the stairs, the very walls tremble.

"Are you scared of the trains?" Ruth asked when the noise had stopped.

"Not really. I got used to them. Jus' stay outta the way. Do they scare you?"

Ruth nodded. The great monsters terrified her, several times a day. She remembered the terror of the flood, then the terror of the fiery face, now the terror of the trains, rattling the house as they spewed out steam and dirty smoke and thundering noise.

After awhile Marie said, "Gotta go take my water home and help my ma get supper. I was sure pleasured to come into your house. It's so warm and clean." When Marie left, she was very happy, for Mama had sent some milk home with her

It had been such fun playing paper dolls with Marie. Now she played with her new catalog paper dolls alone, but it was not nearly as much fun with Marie gone. It was kind of like when Ophelia left. Feeding the chickens and finding eggs was not so much fun by herself. Perhaps Marie would come again. Perhaps she could help to take the place of her lost almost-sister who went away.

Other neighbors dropped by. Ophelia's big brother stopped by to see if they needed anything.

"Hello, Mr. Blankenbuckler!" Daddy greeted him.

"No need to call me Blankenbuckler. That's too much name. Everybody calls me Bob Blank, or just Bob for short."

Daddy showed him the new floor. He liked it. "Wish my mama could have had it so good when she lived here," he said. He picked Ruth up and carried her for a piggy back ride up the path to barn. Then he found in his pocket a stick of Wrigley's Spearmint Gum and handed it to Ruth. She was delighted, but too shy to say thank you. Something was wrong with his eyes. One of them always looked straight ahead.

After he left, Ruth asked, "Daddy, why did one of his eyes never move? It was so strange."

"Sometime long ago he lost one eye. Maybe he got hurt in an accident. So he bought an artificial glass eye to put in its place."

Ruth asked no more, but she thought about the different neighbors. Ed Russell was gruff and dirty with tobacco stains on his mouth, and well, so much like a fierce bear. Bob Blank was merry and kind even though he had a glass eye. She hoped Bob Blank would come again

Perhaps he might even bring another stick of gum.

CHAPTER 5

CHRISTMAS

1927

One morning in December, Ruth awoke to a dazzling new world of white. Frost ferns edged the windows, like lace. A few flakes of white were floating down on the newness and brightness.

"Look at the sugar, Daddy!"

"That's just what I said when I was little. But it's not sugar. It's snow, and it's lots of fun. We're going sledding. I've made a sled for you for Christmas, and we'll just break it in a little early. Come and see it."

Daddy brought the new sled up on the back porch. Ruth had never seen anything like it. The platform had long smooth bars underneath. Daddy showed her where she would sit, and how the wooden runners would slide over the snow.

"Let's try it now!" she said.

After a breakfast of cornmeal mush and sweet milk, they wrapped up in coats and scarves and mittens and wool caps and rubber overshoes, until only their faces were showing. Soon they all set out for the hill in the cow pasture. Her parents took turns pulling the new sled uphill. At the top of the hill, Daddy gave Ruth a gentle push, and she flew over the crispy, crunchy snow. The sky was so blue and bright. The earth was so white and bright. She squinted her eyes almost shut. She held her mittens over her face for the wind stung and burned, even inside her nose as she breathed. She was flying between the bright earth and the bright sky.

"Do it again!" Over and over she coasted down till they were all so cold they had to go back home. Glittering white clumps of snow covered everything ugly. Even the chugging of the train seemed muffled, softer and gentler, further away and less scary. Today she lived in a magic wonderland.

"We must do one more thing before we go inside," said Mama. She picked up a handful of snow and clumped it into a ball, then rolled it in the snow until it grew bigger and bigger. They all rolled balls. Daddy stopped his biggest one just outside the kitchen porch. He put Mama's ball on top of his, and Ruth's little ball on the very top. He stuck a stick between the two top balls, and gave Ruth some wood chips.

"Put these on the top ball to make eyes and nose and mouth," he said. And there stood a funny fat man with stick arms. Ruth laughed and laughed at the wonderful snowman. Then they stomped the snow off their rubber overshoes and shook it off their coats and went inside. They smelled the delicious potatoes and kusha squash and parsnips that Mama had put into the oven to bake before they went sledding. Mama brought in a bowl of her home made butter, frozen solid in the old kitchen. They carved out the hard butter, and spread it on the hot mealy vegetables. As Ruth savored the flavors she thought nothing could ever be better.

But when they had eaten every scrap of the baked food, Mama said, "We're going to have something else you've never had before, Ruth. Snow has lots of surprises, even if it's not sugar like you first thought." Mama took three bowls and went outside. She brought them back filled with clean snow. Over each bowl she poured fresh cream, and sprinkled sugar on top.

"Snow cream!" She handed out the bowls. Ruth tasted it-- such creamy cold sweetness, as it melted on her tongue. She had to eat it slowly because it was so cold, but she had to eat it fast because it was already beginning to melt. What wonders the snow had brought, and that was not the end.

"This snow gives me the Christmas spirit," said Daddy. He took his axe and soon brought home a cedar from their woods. Ruth watched as he set it up in the living room. The top bent over as it touched the ceiling. The tree filled most of one side of the room. The fresh woodsy smell and the green branches made it seem like they had brought the forest inside.

Mama folded and cut a piece of white paper. Ruth unfolded the paper; it had become a lacy snowflake. Mama folded and cut another piece of paper. It had become a lacy hanging basket. Mama put a walnut in the bottom to make it stretch out long for the pretty lace to show and she hung it on the tree. They cut paper chains, dolls,

"It's wonderful. I never saw anything like it."

angels, and lanterns and more snowflakes and baskets. Mama poured a layer of popcorn in a fine wire cage and shook it back and forth over the red coals in the fireplace until the screen box was bursting with fluffy white kernels. She showed Ruth how to thread a needle and sew the popcorn into long chains. They hung the beautiful chains and lacy cutouts on the tree, and spread over all fluffy wisps of cotton snow. It was like a dream, except it wasn't. It was really real, a glorious tree.

The Russell girls came over to see the marvelous tree: Marie, Tansy, Juanita, Edna, Beatrice, and Maxine. "It's wonderful. I never saw anything like it."

"Sit down girls," said Mama. "Did you ever hear the story of why folks have Christmas trees?"

"Not really. Not much Christmas in this valley. Sure not at our house."

Mama told the girls the manger story of Jesus birth.

"I like your story, Mis Rister. I ain't never heard many stories outa the Bible. I hear it's a mighty good book," said Marie.

"It is! Girls, if you'd like more stories, come over sometime. On Friday night and Saturday we sit around the fire and tell a lot of Bible stories, and sing."

"I'll sure come if my pa and ma will let me," said Marie. "This is so wonderful—the tree, and the story, and all. My father would never let us have anything so grand as this," said Marie.

"You mean—he doesn't want you to have pretty things?"

"Oh, my no. Don't dare even ask. Let me tell you what happened once when Lloyd dared ask. He went with Pa to Cresses store over on the highway. Lloyd's overalls was nothing but tatters. He spied a new pair for $1.29, and said, 'Pa, hit shore would be nice to have me this pair of overalls.' Pa got so mad to think Lloyd would dare ask such a thing, he took two dollar bills out of his pocket, opened the door on the heater stove, and threw 'em in on the coals. Lloyd was jus' as quick. He grabbed the money out afore it could burn up. Hit was only scorched on the edges. He gave the money to Mr. Cress and got his overalls."

"I'm so sorry," Mama said. "Do you ever get a chance to earn a little money yourself so you can buy a few things?"

"He grabbed the money afore it could burn up."

"Well—yes and no. Sometimes in the spring or summer Mike gets Lloyd or me to take our one eyed mule to plow. Her name's Betsy. We plow his whole field and he gives us a quarter for a day's work. But quick as we get home, my pa takes it so he can buy him some likker. We never get a penny of it. Hain't no use for us to work, but if Mike wants us to plow, my pa would beat us up if we don't go. He gets mean as a bunch of hornets if we ever cross him in any way."

That was when Mama started cutting up every worn out garment to piece crazy quilts for the poor neighbors.

Christmas morning there was a little box wrapped in brown paper lying underneath the tree.

Mama said, "Look! This box has your name on it! Better see what's inside!"

Ruth pulled off the string and paper and found a peculiar contraption inside. There was a curved tin eye piece, edged in brown velvet. The tin eye piece was fastened to a long narrow board with a handle under it.

"Hold it up to your eyes, like this," said Mama. Ruth took hold of the handle and put the curved metal piece over her eyes, just as her mother had done. There were two tiny windows to look through. Mama put a picture card in the wire rack on top of the wooden part.

"Now look at the picture!" Ruth saw Joseph and Mary, carrying the baby Jesus on a donkey with an angel guarding them. But the people and the angel seemed to stand out from the background of trees and sky, just as if they were alive and ready to move. Ruth laughed, "They're alive!"

Mama gave her another card and then another from a whole pack of cards. "It's a new invention called a stereoscope," she said.

Ruth felt so tingly and happy inside. Then she remembered how Marie said she had nothing like this magical tree in her cold cabin.

"Mama, could I take my new stereoscope over to Marie and let her see it? And maybe some surprises for her family too?"

"Of course. Run down to the cellar and get a jar of peaches."

Mama took a basket and they put in the jar of peaches, a jar of milk, a jar of cottage cheese, a cake of fresh butter and some sweet potatoes. They put on their wraps and set out for Marie's cabin, just across the railroad and road.

The log house had no foundation except a pile of smooth stones under each corner. The yard of hard packed clay was muddy and slippery, with no shrubs or bushes of any kind.

The girls saw them and came running to the door and invited them in. They climbed up the steps to the porch and entered a room so dark at first Ruth could not see anything except the tiny fire burning in the hearth. Then she saw the dingy newspapers pasted over the logs, and a huge framed photograph over the fireplace. Three wooden chairs with broken down cane seats sat in front of the fire. Crude bed frames stood in both corners, each with a pile of filthy rags for covers. One door opened into an even darker bedroom and another into a meager kitchen with a dirt floor.

"Brought you a little something for Christmas!" said Mama. "And Ruth wants you to see her new toy."

Ruth showed the girls her stereoscope, and they laughed and marveled at the almost-alive pictures. When they saw the peaches and milk and other goodies in the basket they almost yelled, "We'll have a feast!"

Retha Russell, the mother, stood there staring at the bounty, and then at her visitors. Her thin body looked like it would topple over with a tiny breeze and her dirty ragged dress did little to give any warmth. Her stringy hair was knotted up on the back of her head. Finally she said, "You are good people. I don't know how to thank you. We usually have skillet corn bread or light bread biscuits once in awhile."

"Is that all you have to eat?"

"Well, sometimes Ed shoots us a rabbit or squirrel or even a possum. We try to make the pork last as long as we can when we butcher a hog in the fall. But it's all gone already this year."

Marie said, "Mis Rister, would you tell my ma the Christmas story, like you told us?"

"Sure. Be happy to." And Mama told the manger story again. Everyone sat or stood listening without moving. "We have more stories like this every Saturday and singing too. Would you and the girls like to come over and hear more?"

The girls saw them coming and came running.

"That would be wonderful. I'll ask Ed if they can come."

After Ruth and her mother returned home, it seemed like a palace, so clean and warm and cozy. "Mama, this is such a wonderful Christmas. You know what the best part is?"

"What?"

"Taking a basket of goodies to Marie and her family. They have so little and it was such fun to share with them. We have so much."

CHAPTER 6

LIZZIE'S PROBLEM

1928

January was cold, rainy, and windy. Daddy said it was raw weather. One blustery day he said, "Our new floor and stove help, but there is still a lot of heat that escapes through that stairwell. I'm going to make a trapdoor to close off the top of the stairs and keep it even warmer here in our new kitchen. Tomorrow I'll go to Sienknecht's to get the lumber."

"Great idea, Knudt! You are working hard to make our house comfortable. I sure do appreciate it. God has given us a warm house and plenty of water in our well just outside the back porch," said Mama.

The next day Daddy prepared to go to Oliver Springs. After a few minutes he came back inside.

"You won't believe this," he said. "I tried to start Lizzie. I turned the crank over and over as always, and nothing happened. So I lifted the hood, and there as plain as day, was a hole in the engine where the generator should be. I guess somebody thought they needed it worse than we do—or they wanted to sell it to somebody else who needs one."

"Just think, it was parked right outside our house. They sure were quiet and sneaky to take out the generator while we were asleep."

"Wonder what kind of neighbors we have anyhow."

"Daddy, I think we need to plant a lot of seeds for Jesus," said Ruth.

"You are absolutely right."

After the discovery of Lizzie's trouble, everyone was quiet for a while.

"Daddy, what will we do now?"

46

"Just like the neighbors do, Ruth. Walk, or hitch up Meg and Peg to the buggy or wagon."

The room was quiet again, except for an occasional crackle from the fireplace. But the peace as usual was gone. A thief had stolen it when he took Lizzie's generator away.

"Think I'll walk down the tracks and go talk to Bob Blank," said Daddy.

"May I go too?" Ruth had memories of Spearmint Gum dancing in her head.

"Sure. Bundle up. Wind is fierce."

Shortly the two began walking to the neighbor's house on the railroad track. The gravel and wooden ties made the best kept road in the valley. Everybody walked the tracks to go anywhere. Ruth tried walking the rail, balancing herself with arms held straight out like a bird flying. Far down the tracks they could see the cloudy curly white smoke rising from the Blank's chimney. In a few minutes they saw the two story house, weathered clapboard like their own except it had no front porch and wasn't snuggled down in cozy bushes. It looked like a giant cold box.

Myrtle Blank invited them in.

"Come, sit by the fire and warm your cold hands." Mrs. Blankenbuckler was a large, motherly woman. She wore a blue bib apron over her flour sack dress. Her brown hair was coiled in a roll on the back of her head.

Bob Blank poked around in the cupboards, and found a stick of gum. He handed it to Ruth with a grin, "For my little red-topped peanut. How are you folks doing up there? Keeping warm enough? Got food enough?"

"We are fine. Your mother left us plenty of food for the winter in the cellar and the kushas and sweet potatoes and onions and beans she had stored and dried for the winter. But we do have a big problem. Can't drive our tin Lizzie. Somebody stole her generator last night."

"Might a-knowed, somebody was gonna' cash in on that purty Model T sittin' there like a possum playin' possum," said Bob. "Them Model T's so popular they can sell your generator real easy. Some of them's been trying to fish out your story from me. They want to know if you paid cash for the place, how much and all that. I jus' tell them the business was between you and my father, not me. I sure hate it my neighbors gone and done you like that."

"Do you have any idea where I can buy another generator? Is there a shop in Oliver Springs that sells car parts?"

"Well, now, Tom Abston got a garage on the corner of Kingston and Winters Gap. You know, where you get your gas. He's got a few car parts. He might could help you."

"You know, where you get your gas."

"I'll try Tom Abston then. Appreciate your help."

Myrtle Blank started to talk next. "Don't go yet. Get this little girl warm first. Mind if I ask you a question?"

"Sure, go ahead and ask."

"Folks jus' cain't figure you all out. When they hear you all are from Kentucky, hit's like you come from a foreign land. Most folks make it to Oliver Springs only once or twice a year. Another thing they cain't figure out is that you don't roll cigarettes, don't dip snuff, don't chaw chawing tobacco, don't drink likker. Tell me, what do you do to pleasure yourself?"

"Well, I guess you might think I really am strange when I tell you how I do pleasure myself. I like to read. Now you must think I'm absolutely crazy!"

"Strange, maybe, but wonderful. How I wish I could read. I never had enough schoolhousing to read much of anything. Tell me, what do you learn?"

"News of course. What is happening in the world, what President Coolidge is doing in Washington, and such. But I have one favorite Book I read every day that I like even better. You may have heard of it."

"What book is that?"

"It's called the Bible. It has a lot better news than the newspapers."

"I thought the Bible was very old. How can it have news in it?"

"Well, you know all the wicked things people do to-day—like stealing my generator. The Bible says all these wicked things are a sign of Jesus coming, and that He is coming soon."

"You got it right, Mr. Rister, to read your Bible like that. I don't go to church much. Wish I could read the Bible myself. I believe you're doing what's right to not smoke and chew tobacco. I never did like to empty them filthy spittoons anyhow."

"If you like, come up to our house and I'll read some for you. We read it every day."

Ruth and her father bundled up again and walked the tracks back home. Ruth chewed slowly on one quarter of her treasured gum stick; the other three fourths she held tightly in her pocket. She wasn't afraid of the trains since she was with Daddy, but she was glad when they got home. She didn't like the trains. Every day, as an engine came closer and closer, it chugged and chugged with ter-rible thunder as it came up the grade toward their house. The giant round face glared at her like an evil eye. Black dirty smoke and cinders billowed upward from the black smokestack. It roared past the house, an enormous monster, louder and louder and bigger and bigger until the thunder filled the house and nobody could talk or even think. It never jumped off the tracks and came up to the house but it sure sounded like it would devour them alive. Then all the rest of the train followed: freight cars, coal cars, tank cars, flat cars, and finally the red caboose.

The next morning Daddy hitched Meg and Peg to the farm wagon. Ruth did not even ask to go. It would be no fun to ride for hours with bitter wind biting her nose and cheeks. Mama gave Daddy a hot stone wrapped in newspaper to lay at his feet, and wrapped him in a blanket over his heavy mackinaw and wool cap and mittens.

Toward evening Daddy drove Meg and Peg up beside the back porch and tied the horses to a post. He came inside to warm himself before unloading the boards for the trapdoor from the wagon.

"Did you get your generator?" Ruth asked.

"Tom Abston didn't have one. But he sent a telegram from the train depot, to Knoxville. Should be here in a couple of weeks, he said. Road sure is getting washed out. It's so muddy in places I was afraid the wheels would mire down. We probably can't take many more trips to town till spring in Lizzie or the wagon. But surprise! I found some treats: an orange for each of us, and a lemon. Now, Emma, we can have davla."

Mama looked pleased and said she would cook davla the very next day, which she did. First she set her black iron pot in the stove hole directly over the fire. Next she poured into it a gallon of sweet milk, and began to stir it with a wooden spoon.

"So the milk won't scorch and taste burned," she said. She stood and stirred so long that Ruth quit watching.

Finally Mama said, "It's time. Want to see?" Ruth pulled up a chair and stood on it to watch. The milk had boiled down so there was much less in the pot. Mama poured into it three beaten eggs and the juice of the lemon Daddy had bought. Tiny curds began to form in the milk, then more and more and bigger and bigger curds. Mama lifted the pot off the fire.

Finally Mama said, "It's time. Want to see?"

For supper they ate bowls of the sweet davla curds. Ruth's first bite felt so cool and creamy and delicious, the texture of the cottage cheese Mama made, but not tangy and sour. It was almost like a creamy fruit soup with chunks of applesauce in it. The next bite was even better, and the next and the next. Ruth ate and ate—three bowls full of that wonderful davla, until she could not hold another spoonful.

"This is how they make it in Norway," Mama said. "Everybody from the old country likes davla."

Daddy began to make the trapdoor to close off the empty space in the new kitchen, as they called the dining room where the stove was now set up. Ruth watched him saw the boards he had bought in Oliver Springs. She got her old job back to give him the nails to pound into the crosspieces so it began to look like a door. Then with hinges he screwed the door to the bottom of the ceiling hole above the stairs. To make the trapdoor easy to pull up and down, he fastened a pulley and rope to the high ceiling, with one end of the rope tied around a heavy piece of iron, and the other end coming through a little hole in the door. He showed Ruth how to pull the rope so the door would raise high, and she could go upstairs, and how to let it down gently to close off the cold air space. Now the kitchen would be much warmer.

"We must do something with these scraps of leftover wood," Daddy said. Ruth watched as he made a shallow box and put posts at the corners and fastened a roof over it.

"Is this a little house for my dolls?" asked Ruth.

"No. A house for your new pets!"

"What pets?"

"Just wait a few more minutes." It was hard to be good and patient but she must.

"Now we're going outside. Put on your coat." He carried the house without walls outside. He picked up his post hole digger and a post in his toolshed. He walked on and stopped just outside the dining room window. He set the post hole digger in the ground, bit up a big chunk of dirt and set it aside. He dug up more dirt and more dirt until he had a hole about a foot deep. He picked up the heavy post.

"Now you help me get the post in straight." Ruth held it tightly. He pushed dirt back into the hole around the post and tamped it down firm and tight. Then he nailed the open sided house on top of the post.

"Now ask your mother for some crumbs or corn or chicken feed to put in the tray, and you will see a show! Your new pets are coming!" Ruth did as she was told. Then she settled down on her favorite second stair to watch. A bright red bird with a stand up crest flew in and began to eat the food. Soon a gray bird came, then a brown one, and another and another.

"The birds! They like it!" Ruth clapped her hands.

Every day now the air was cold and colder, and some days the wind blew and tried very hard to force the coldness in through any little crack. But Daddy's new trapdoor invention and the tight floor made the new kitchen cozy and warm. Many days rain beat against the windows and everything outside was soggy and sad. Margie stayed inside and sat on her stair bench to color and look at her books and watch the birds at the feeder her father had made for her just outside the window. She hoped Myrtle Blank would come and listen to Daddy read the Bible, but she never came.

In two weeks Daddy got the generator from Tom Abston and hooked it up to the motor. He drove the Model T across the yard and parked it right under the bedroom window.

"Nobody will dare touch our Lizzie now," he said. "We would hear them from our bed, just a few feet away."

"Now we can go see the peacocks again! I'm glad you got Lizzie fixed, Daddy."

Lizzie's problems were over. For now. It was well that neither Ruth nor Lizzie knew what else was in store.

"Now you help me get the post in straight."

CHAPTER 7

GUARD DUTY

SPRING, 1928

After Christmas passed, the skies were often gray. Instead of bringing bright snow the clouds brought rain to beat against the windows and made the brown grass soggy wet. The cookstove fire chased away the dampness in the kitchen. Ruth sat on her second stair window seat to soak up the coziness. When it stopped raining, she watched the cardinals and chickadees and titmice fly in to eat in her feeder.

On Sabbaths the family stopped work except taking care of the animals. They gathered in front of the fireplace and had their own church service. Daddy tuned the strings on his violin, and played the tune for their songs—a melody sweet, clear and as light and cheery as a sunbeam coming in the window. They sang songs from "Christ in Song", such as "The Lily of the Valley," "Happy Songs," and "How I Wish I Knew." Ruth loved the star song, number 253:

> "Little stars that twinkle in the heaven's blue
> I have often wondered if you ever knew,
> How there 'rose one like you, leading wise old men
> From the East, thro' Judah, down to Bethlehem.
> Did you watch the Saviour all those years of strife?
> Did you know, for sinners, how he gave his life?
> Little stars that twinkle in the heaven's blue,
> All you saw of Jesus how I wish I knew."

She thought of the twinkling stars she could see only at night. They must be kind of like angels; sometimes you see them, sometimes you don't.

Next they studied the Sabbath school lesson. Mama always had the children's story for Ruth. Marie came over to listen as often as her pa would allow. One day she was very quiet after the story about Jesus healing the lepers.

"I wish I could've been there to see those lepers get healed. Jesus must have been a mighty good Man to cure them like that."

"He was a mighty good Man, Marie. He was more than a Man. He was God on earth. No ordinary man could do what He did. And He wants to be your Friend today."

"Really?"

"Really. All you have to do is ask Him to come into your heart."

After Marie had gone home, Ruth said, "Marie likes the Bible stories. Are they joy seeds?"

"Yes, indeed. Perhaps Marie will be the first person to let them sprout and grow in her heart."

"I hope so. I like Marie."

Every day Ruth did the chores together with Mama. First they drew water from the well. Mama carried it inside and set the bucket on the washstand. Then they carried in firewood for the woodboxes. The chickens were next. Ruth learned to toss out their food, and carry a little basket so she could find hidden eggs herself.

One day Mama said, "Ruth, you know how to feed the chickens very well. How would you like to take care of them yourself?"

"Do you really think I could?

"Of course. You know where to find the food and the nests all by yourself."

"I will do that!" So Ruth had her first regular chores. She took a bucket of water and a pan filled with chicken feed and corn. She tossed the feed out on the ground and the fat red hens ran squawking all around her. She began squawking back to them, "Cawk, cawk, cawk!" Next she filled the water pans from her bucket. She took the egg basket and first checked the row of nest boxes in the barn shed. Each box had a shiny porcelain egg lying on the straw nest. The make believe egg was supposed to encourage the hens to lay their eggs there, but they did not always want to, and sometimes hid their nests along the fence. So Ruth checked under all the bushes last. Then she carried her basket of eggs inside for Mama.

Every day that Daddy felt strong enough, he took the axe and set out for the woods. Ruth could not go with him to watch him chop trees on the steep hillsides. But when he had cut off the branches he would snake the long logs down the hill and Ruth could go to watch if she stayed out of the way. He hitched Meg and Peg to a heavy chain and took them up the hill. Then he fastened the chain around the logs and Meg and Peg pulled them down the hill to the woodlot. There he unfastened the load and the horses climbed the hill again to bring another load. He must be very careful or the heavy logs would slide down the hill too fast and crash into the horses. On sunny days he and Mama took a crosscut saw and sawed those logs back and forth and back and forth until they were cut into pieces just the right length for the stove and fireplace. They were beginning to cut the wood supply for the year. The wood would dry out during the summer and be seasoned just right for the next winter.

Every day Mama cooked vegetables. Plenty of mustard greens and kale and turnips still grew in the garden the Blankenbucklers had planted early in the fall. She baked sweet and Irish potatoes, kusha squash and parsnips and whole wheat bread. They ate the good canned food Mrs. Blankenbuckler had left in the cellar: beans, tomatoes, sauerkraut, blackberries, peaches and applesauce. Every day they had fresh milk and cottage cheese and butter and eggs and buttermilk.

Ruth liked to watch Mama cook wheat in the fireless cooker. Mama opened the top of the gray wooden box on the porch. The top was a lid that opened up on hinges. Inside the box was a round hole, made of wire mesh. The space between the sides of the box and the round hole was stuffed tightly with shredded wood, called excelsior.[1]

---

1   Excelsior. Wood shavings or shreds or curls, was the common packing material for fragile items, and for insulation. Used much like the Styrofoam "peanuts" today.

Mama carefully took from the top of the stove the round soapstone[2] she had been heating and put it in the hole in the fireless cooker box. Then she put on top of the hot soapstone the round pot which she had boiling on the stove, full of wheat kernels. Both the soapstone and the round pot fitted exactly in the hole in the box. She stuffed more excelsior over the boiling pot, and closed the lid. The soapstone would stay hot and keep the pot simmering slowly all night. In the morning the wheat kernels would be well cooked, soft and delicious, especially with fresh cream.

Daddy said, "I do believe my pellagra is better. I don't feel as dreadfully tired, and see my hands?"

Ruth looked. Truly the ugly scales and flakes seemed better. "Are you getting well, Daddy?"

"I think so, Little Peach. All the good milk and vegetables are making me strong again. Thank God for our farm and home."

One day Daddy said, "Ground's getting dry enough to plow." He hitched up the horses, and for days they pulled and tugged that heavy iron plowshare through the soil of the main garden and the creek garden. The black earth lay turned over in long furrows. Daddy was tired at the end of a day of such heavy work, but not super-tired as he used to be when the pellagra was bad.

Next he hitched the horses to the harrow. It was a wooden device made like a triangle. Sharp iron spikes stuck out underneath the frame. As Meg and Peg pulled it across the newly plowed soil, the spikes tore up the clods and made the earth soft and crumbly. After they had harrowed the long furrows in one direction, they changed and harrowed it across the other direction. The ground was ready to be planted.

---

2   Soapstone. A kind of talc, a soft rock quarried in large blocks from the in earth. Called soapstone because it feels soapy or oily. Not affected by heat or acid. Used for fireless cookers, lab table tops, French chalk for marking cloth, lining for laundry tubs, furnaces and heating stoves, and insulation for electricity. Talc is ground up to use in talcum powder and face powder, also in paper, crayons, and paint.

Daddy was ready to start the early garden. He laid out a long bed between the fence and the asparagus. He stuck six short sticks at the each end of the bed, and tied a string between the sticks to mark straight rows. He was neat and careful.

"Now we'll plant the onions," he said. Ruth handed him the tiny onion sets and he pushed them in the earth right underneath that long tight string line. Then he moved the string to the next sticks, and Ruth helped plant another straight row.

Later he made the rows for the peas. He set a guide line, and pulled the hoe handle through the earth underneath the string to make a little trench.

"You may help plant the peas." Ruth and Mama each took a handful of the hard greenish seeds and carefully dropped them into the trench he had made. Daddy covered them with soil and tamped them down, safe and snug. After they had made six rows, he put a stick at the end for a sign. "Now, Ruth, you put the seed package on the stick so we will remember what we planted here."

"Sunshine will warm the seeds through the glass."

Daddy cleaned off the grass and weeds from part of the sunny slope behind the house. He took several pieces of board about three feet long, and nailed them together to make frames with no top or bottom. He set these frames on the cleaned off place on the slope and filled them with black garden soil. Ruth helped him spread the soil evenly to make beds for the seeds to sprout and grow.

They carefully planted cabbage and tomato and bell pepper seeds and cut pieces of sweet potatoes, and gently sprinkled them with earth and water. Lastly Daddy laid large pieces of glass over the top of the frames.

"Cold frames, Little Peach. The glass will let in the sunshine to warm the seeds and keep out the frost so they won't freeze. We'll have baby plants much sooner than if we planted them in the garden without the cold frames."

"Will they grow up big in these boxes?"

"No, this is just to start them. When the weather is warmer we'll transplant the baby plants to the garden."

One morning some time later Daddy said, "I'm going to harrow the creek garden. It's time we got the Irish potatoes planted."

He whistled as he hitched up Peg and Meg to the harrow again. The horses dragged it to the creek garden and began to break up the rough furrows there. Ruth followed to play beside the creek. She squished down the wiry stems of a clump of bulrushes to make a cushion and sat down to soak up the sunshine and sweet spring smells.

A crow flew overhead scolding "Caw, caw, caw." She picked a tiny new mint leaf and chewed its sweetness. It was too cold for much mint to grow now, but the watercress was green all winter, floating in a clump in the water. She nibbled on a tangy sprig of watercress. It reminded her of little green onions. Tiny silver minnows darted about in the sparkly water at her feet. She poked a stone with a stick; a crawfish dashed away for a new hiding place. Ruth got up from her bulrush cushion and started home across the roughly plowed garden. Daddy was at the far end, ordering the horses to turn right. "Gee,

Meg, Gee, Peg. Slowly now, turn around. Now Giddy up, giddy up." And they started back toward her.

Ruth looked at the horses. It would be a long time before they pulled that heavy harrow to where she was. She had plenty of time to run home across the garden in front of them. She began to run, but tripped over one of the chunky clods of dirt, right in the path of the horses, and the sharp spikes of the harrow. She struggled to get up but just couldn't move. But she knew Daddy would see her and stop the horses.

But Daddy did NOT see her. He did NOT call "Whoa!" to Meg and Peg. The horses kept right on coming straight toward her. In a moment they came to where she lay, trying to get up, but seemed to be helpless and powerless to move. Both Meg and Peg gently stepped over her with their front feet and stopped dead still.

Daddy was pushing down hard on the harrow and watching to be sure he was breaking up the hard clods. He did not see his little girl lying motionless under the horses, only a few feet from the deadly spikes of the harrow. He yelled, "Giddy up!" to the horses but they refused to budge. He yelled again, but the horses understood the danger and for the first time ever they would not obey. Daddy again ordered them to move on. He reached down to grasp the reins so he could slap their behinds and get them going again. As he did so, he looked up and turned pale. He saw his little girl lying there under the horses legs.

"Whoa!" He yelled to the wise horses, and rushed to help Ruth get up from the ground. He brushed the dirt from her dress and grabbed her tight and said, "Your angel certainly made those horses stand still! You could have been killed by the horses' feet and harrow spikes! Thank the Lord you are safe! Your angel certainly was on guard duty!"

Ruth ran home across the garden. She did not stumble and fall again. How she wished she could have seen her angel stopping Meg and Peg and making them stand very still over her. When Marie came to get her bucket of water, Ruth must tell her.

"You could have been killed by the horses' feet and harrow spikes!"

"Come into the living room. I want to show you something."

Ruth led her friend to the angel picture that Mama had hung on the wall. The picture showed two little children, gathering flowers, trying to catch a butterfly. Without looking ahead, they had no idea they were on the edge of a rocky cliff, and would fall over the edge the next step or two. But behind them was their guardian angel, ready to keep them safe.

"See how the angel is guarding those children, and keeping them safe? That's what my guardian angel did for me today!"

"You mean you were in danger, and your angel took care of you?"

"I was in such danger that I would have been killed if my angel hadn't stopped the horses." And Ruth told the story to Marie and how everybody has a guardian angel.

Marie was amazed. "You mean—everybody has a guardian angel? Even me?"

"Even you. Of course!"

"Now I think I understand. When I come over here to listen to Bible stories my pa gives me a terrible licking, sometimes with his leather horse whip. But somehow I'm able to stand it. Sometimes I feel like it doesn't even hurt. Maybe that's my angel helping me."

For evening prayers that night they talked about how some people had seen angels with their own eyes when they needed help, like Joshua and Mary and Joseph and Peter. But usually folks never see their angels and don't even know they are there.

"Angels are kind of like the stars, Mama. You never see them in the day, and you wouldn't ever know they are there. But sometimes you can see them—at night. They are like the angels. You don't see them, but sometimes when you really need them, they are there for you."

CHAPTER 8

MARKET DAYS

SPRING AND SUMMER, 1928

The cold dark winter was over. Warm bright days made the peas and onion sets send up baby leaves. The tiny shoots in the cold frame grew very fast. Now Ruth was busy every day, helping to plant beets and carrots, lettuce and mustard and kale, parsnips and lima beans, corn and black eye peas, watermelons, cantaloupes, cucumbers, parsley, green beans and pumpkins and kusha squashes. They transplanted the baby plants from the cold frames into the garden and Ruth poured a half cup of water on each baby plant because they had disturbed its roots when they moved it.

Every day Ruth liked to see if any new seeds had sprouted and poked tiny baby shoots through the ground. It took longer for some seeds to sprout than others, especially if it did not rain often. One day she saw only a few beans were coming up.

"Daddy, what happened to all the beans? Very few are coming up."

"Maybe some crows got hungry and ate them. Maybe not enough rain. We'll plant them again." And they did, that very day. They covered the row with mulch so birds would not eat the seeds.

One morning Ruth saw her father tying some old rags on a long pole. She watched him pour some coal oil on the rags.

"What are you doing?"

"Come and see." He carried the pole to the apple trees that grew near the barn. He struck a match and lit the rags and then held the blazing pole up to a white web high in the tree. The stringy white nest burned up in a few seconds. There were more nests, and he burned them up too.

"Tent caterpillars. They are pupas that hatched out from eggs laid last summer, and they spun these silky webs that look almost like tents."

"Why do you burn them?"

"Because they will eat the tiny leaves as soon as they come out. One nest like these can eat up all the leaves on a tree. There are codling moths too that eat right into the baby apples. But we can't burn them off."

Another day she noticed that weeds were growing thickly in the garden.

"Daddy, the weeds are growing faster than the carrot and beet seeds we planted."

"You are right. Let's get rid of the weeds." He chopped with the hoe as closely as he could to the tiny carrots and beets. "Can't get all the weeds out with the hoe. We have to get down on the ground on our knees and pull out the rest." It was hard work to kneel down on the ground and pull weeds, especially with the hot sun beating down on your back. Ruth didn't pull too many. She didn't want to fight all the garden enemies and she would rather play in her favorite spot, underneath the lilac bushes. Ophelia had been right about the flow-

The stringy white nests burned up in a few seconds.

ers that would come up there in the spring. Purple and white violets covered the ground under the bushes. The blossom smells of the lilacs and violets and mock orange filled the air with sweetness.

She watched a mockingbird fly straight up in the air, sing just for fun, and drop back to his tree perch. Far away she heard the faint "Coo, coo, coo," of a mourning dove.

When she took her water and corn out to feed the chickens that day, she noticed Leonie, one of the fat red hens, acting very strangely. She asked Mama, "Why is one hen spreading out her wings and fluffing out her feathers over and over again?"

"She knows it's spring, and she wants to raise a family. We will give her a setting of eggs in a quiet corner of the barn shed. She will sit on the eggs for three weeks, and the baby chicks will hatch out." Every day Ruth took the patient hen food and water. She would get off her nest just long enough to eat and drink, then would turn over her eggs with her beak and gently sit back down on them. The three weeks seemed to never end, but finally one day Ruth saw an eggshell on the straw. When Leonie got off the nest to eat and drink, there were three fluffy yellow chicks. Two more were still wet from just crawling out of their eggshells. Two eggs had little holes where the baby inside was pecking its way out. After they were all hatched, Ruth watched the balls of yellow fluff follow closely to their mother. She wanted so much to cuddle the cute babies in her hands, but she would be good and leave them alone. She remembered Daddy's story of how he accidentally squeezed one to death when he was a little boy and how sad he was when he saw it would never run again. But it was fun to watch the little family checking out together every place the mother hen scratched. She clucked and the chicks peeped and stayed so close they looked like a cloud moving together.

First the new lettuce and new onions were ready to eat. Then the new peas.

They sat on the back porch and shelled the tender new peas.

"We're going to take some of our vegetables to Oliver Springs to sell," said Daddy. They picked the fresh tender lettuce and onions and radishes; they cut new asparagus and mustard and kale, and wrapped them in soft moist pieces of cloth to keep them fresh. They packed them into woven market baskets. They sat together on the back porch and shelled the tender new peas. Mama put in the baskets several jars of her fresh cottage cheese, sour cream, and butter, and boxes of eggs. They loaded the baskets in Lizzie, and drove off to Oliver Springs. Behind the cluster of stores, they stopped at the white and brick houses on Estabrook Avenue. Mama went to the houses and offered their cheese and vegetables to the people liv-

"I have vegetables for you."

ing there. Ruth liked to go to the doors too, even though she was afraid to say a word.

"Good morning!" Mama would say. "I'm Emma Risetter. I live out in Hen Valley. I have fresh vegetables and cottage cheese for you. What would you like? "

"Well, how nice to have a farm woman bring us fresh vegetables! Yes, indeed, I'll take some of everything you have," said the lady at the door.

Before very long everything in the baskets was sold. They made one more stop at Sienknecht's and bought more seeds to plant and feed for the chickens and stock and three oranges for a treat. Ruth gazed at the tall glass jars of striped red and white candy and rainbow colored gum drops, but she would be a good girl and not ask for any.

As the weeks passed, they kept on taking vegetables to market and got to know some of the people living in Oliver Springs. The people liked the door delivery of fresh farm vegetables.

Ruth kept watching for the peacocks at the Harvey Hannah mansion. Finally her mother asked one her customers, Mrs. Ladd, "My little girl keeps asking about those peacocks at the Harvey Hannah house. Do you know their story?"

"Oh yes. Gorgeous, aren't they? Well Colonel Hannah brought them for watchdogs. If anybody comes around that has no business there, they set up a scream and alarm better than any dog. Just like guineas."

"If your little girl wants to know about Harvey Hannah, let me tell you a story about when he was a little boy." She looked straight at Ruth and smiled.

"When Harvey was a little boy he loved to make speeches. When he went to church, he would try to remember everything the preacher said. Then Sunday afternoon he would gather his friends around him and play church. He would preach the sermon as well as he could. He grew up to be a great speaker. Even ran for governor himself. Now he's State Railroad Commissioner and spends most of his time in Nashville. We folks at Oliver Springs are so proud of our own famous Harvey Hannah!"

Sometimes Mama offered one of our customers a book or paper about the Bible. One lady said, "I go to the Baptist Church, and that's good enough for me." Another said, "I go to Harvey Hannah's church, and I like it there."

Another day Mama learned a story about how a traveling preacher had brought in extra religion by speaking in tongues. Then another preacher came from New River, who even handled live rattlesnakes to try to prove he was saved and holy.

"Looks like it's going to be hard to plant joy seeds in Oliver Springs," Mama said one day. "They like the churches they already have. They didn't even listen to the tongues preacher and the rattlesnake preacher, so there's not much chance of their listening to us."

Ruth said, "How are joy seeds ever going to grow if nobody wants them? Marie's the only one who even wants to listen to Bible stories."

"It's like our garden. Takes a lot of time and work. Most important, takes God's sunshine and rain to makes the seeds grow."

Every day they feasted on their fresh vegetables themselves. Daddy was much better; his hands looked almost smooth. The vegetables were helping him to get well from the dreadful pellagra.

The days grew hot and hotter; long and longer. The air stood still and the sun baked down on the ground and growing things. On market days, everyone was busy picking and washing and wrapping the vegetables for market.

They kept on fighting the garden pests. Sometimes Daddy sprayed the beans or other vegetables for beetles and such.

One day Daddy said, "Bugs are eating up the potato vines. Best thing to do is to pick them off. We'll all work together." He gave Ruth a can with some coal oil in it and showed her how to turn over each leaf, looking for the bugs: five black stripes on a yellow back. When she found one she put it in the coal oil to get rid of it.

"Watch for the clusters of yellow eggs too, like this," said Mama. "And the reddish orange red larvae. " All of these they dropped in the coal oil to get rid of the pests. Ruth did not like to pick off the squishy larvae. She did not like the strong smell of the coal oil. Soon she stopped to rest in the shade of the grape arbor.

Another day Ruth and her mother were gathering to-matoes. "What happened? Look at all the holes."

"Turtles," said Mama. " Our turtles might be very old—even a hundred years old, because they can live longer than any other animal, so we'll take good care of them, and even share our tomatoes with them if they want."

"Here's one, Mama!" Ruth had found the tomato-eat-er, shut up tight in the hard shell of his box house.

"Fine. I'll carry him down to the creek meadow and he can eat the grasses there instead of our tomatoes."

When the corn was beginning to get tall, Daddy said, "Another enemy to fight. Smut on the corn."

"What's smut?" asked Ruth.

"Black stuff that grows on the corn. Looks like soot. It will grow bigger and kill the plant. Have to cut it out and burn it." Ruth helped Daddy find the weird boil-looking growths on the corn. He cut them out and carried them away and burned them.

Then the apples were ripe. Many were partly rotten or bored into by worms, but they gathered them in buckets and baskets and set them on the back porch. They all sat in chairs to work up the apples. Ruth scoured off the black fungus spots with a brush and water and washed them clean. They cut out the wormy holes and peeled and sliced them in thin slices and dropped the pieces in salt water so they would not turn brown. Ruth could do the next job. She dipped the apples out of the salt water and spread them on wide racks. Mama set the racks in the sunshine to dry. It was an easy job, sitting on the cool shady porch, except for the neighbors that smelled the sweetness and flew in to suck up the feast of juice. There were honey bees, flies, yellow jackets, wasps, mud daubers, and tiny gnats flying around together to get close to the cut apples. One time Ruth got stung by a yellow jacket and Mama had to pull out the stinger and daub a paste of soda and water on the painful spot.

Ruth remembered the dried apples they had eaten last winter. Mama had cooked those Mrs. Blankenbuckler had dried last summer. Their new dried apples would mean more applesauce next winter. She ate a crunchy thin slice. Better than candy, any day!

That day Mama cooked succotash and potatoes. Ruth asked, "Could we have sour cream gravy on our potatoes?"

"Of course. Want to watch?" Ruth pulled her chair up close to the stove. Mama poured sour cream into the iron skillet, and stirred it as it heated. Soon tiny bubbles rose to the top and burst and then the cream separated into small clumps and browned. Mama put in some flour and stirred it smooth, then added sweet milk.

They sat down to eat that delicious dinner. Daddy said the grace, and Ruth began tasting the creaminess of the potatoes and sour cream gravy, the sweetness of the tender green beans, the crunchiness of the corn dodgers and the fresh radishes and lettuce. The succotash of corn and onions and okra and tomatoes was like a dessert; the onions and tomatoes had flavored each other just right; the okra and corn tasted much better than if they were cooked separately.

"Like it, Little Peach?"

Ruth nodded. Anybody would like succotash, and sour cream gravy, and all the other goodies they had to eat!

"Remember how we had to work to help these good things to grow?"

Ruth nodded again. "You mean, how we had to take the turtles out of the tomatoes, and replant the beans, and pick the bugs off the potatoes, and pull the weeds and cut out the smut, and all that?"

"Right. It was a lot of work, and took a lot of time. Of course, God really did the growing. Now we're eating delicious food, almost like a celebration. Here's a riddle for you: What else are we working on that's like a garden? Takes a lot of work and time and God really does the growing?"

"I know! Joy seeds!"

"You guessed it! Remember what your part is?"

"Yes, Daddy, I remember. I'll keep working hard on my memory verses."

Ruth helped Daddy find the weird black growths on the corn.

CHAPTER 9

WILD HARVEST

SUMMER, 1928

"Hope we don't get a blackberry winter," Daddy said one day in the spring when the weather turned nippy cold.

"What's a blackberry winter?" asked Ruth.

"Sometimes in the spring, when the white blossoms cover the brambles like they do now, a cold snap may freeze the tender flowers and they cannot grow any fruit that year. We need the berries for food for the winter. And of course a blackberry cobbler or two. Want to go berrying with us this summer, Little Peach?"

"Oh, yes! May I go, Daddy?"

"Of course! But I must warn you. It won't be easy. There'll be enemies to fight, just like when we grow a garden."

"What kind of enemies? We don't weed the wild berry bushes, or pick bugs off them."

"Tiny ones. Flying and creeping. Hot sun. Can you fight those enemies?"

"Sure. I'm not afraid of bugs and sunshine."

"Then we better get you ready to fight," said Mama. "We must order you little overalls to wear."

"But girls don't wear overalls! They're for boys!"

"Yes, I know. Women and girls don't wear pants, but that's the only sensible thing to do when you pick berries. They will help to fight the chiggers and prickers." They got out the Sears Roebuck catalog and found a picture of a little boy's overalls, and ordered the size that would fit a little girl.

Once a week they made the long trip to the corner to check the mailbox. Finally her package came. Ruth opened it up and tried on the little overalls. It felt strange to wear pants, like a man. Now if only the berries would hurry and get ripe.

Ruth kept watching the berry brambles next to Strawberry Hill. The hard green berries grew longer and larger, and turned red, and finally they were very long and turned black. One day she found some juicy ripe ones.

"I found some sweet berries on our brambles! How soon can we go berry picking?"

"Put on your new overalls. Let's go this morning," Daddy said.

First Ruth put her overalls on over her dress. Then she put on her high topped boots and tucked the pants legs inside the boots.

"Now you're ready to fight most bugs," said Mama. "We'll have to do more to fight chiggers. Rub some of this coal oil on your boot tops and the edges of the pants tucked into the boots, and around your dress collar and cuffs and wrists."

Even though chiggers were bright red they were so tiny you could scarcely see them. Ruth had seen them the time they dug in around her waist and under her arms. They made raised bumps on her skin and stayed there, itching and burning, till Marie came over and dug them out with her fingernails. Marie said you could paint over the bumps with fingernail polish. Then the chiggers couldn't get any air and they would suffocate. So Ruth was glad to put on the coal oil even though the smell was horrible and the fumes almost made her choke. Last of all she put on her wide brimmed straw hat to protect her from getting sunburned by the hot summer sun. Mama put on a pair of Daddy's overalls, and did the coal oil trick too. So did Daddy. They were ready.

Ruth took her bucket and followed her mother and father to the berry brambles. It was easy to pick from the lower canes; just reach out and grab the juicy black berries and drop them in her bucket. But even though the overalls protected her from the thorns and tiny chiggers crawling on the bushes, there were other things to watch for. Flying bugs flitted back and forth, searching for the ripest berries, and then sat down to suck the sweet juice: bumblebees, yellow jackets, wasps, mud daubers, and gnats. She had to be careful that she didn't pick a berry that had already been claimed by a bug, and get stung by the insect fighting for its berry rights. She also tried to watch that when she picked a berry she did not pull off the stem from which it hung, for who wanted to eat berry stems along with their berries. Sometimes leaves would fall into the bucket too, or she would get a small unripe berry and that should also be thrown out. To pick a bucket full of clean ripe berries was much better than to pick one that had lots of stems, leaves, or unripe berries in it, for all those things would have to be cleaned when they got back home.

By now it was July and the ground and the grass and trees sizzled from the baking sun. Sometimes it was so hot Ruth saw heat waves shimmering in the air above the ground as the heat rose. Being safe from the chiggers and thorns inside the overalls didn't protect her from the heat, and she got very hot and soon sweat was running down her face, her back, and her whole body. Ruth had to stop after awhile and rest under her favorite oak tree that she loved to climb.

The next day Ruth went berrying again with her parents, down to The Forty. They carried their buckets and walked down the narrow dirt road to their other farm, which was only forty acres. Part of the way the road simply was Hen Valley Creek bed, and they jumped from one stone to another to avoid getting their feet wet. The water was very shallow, so there was no danger of falling in or drowning.

When they reached The Forty they crossed the meadow where the grass was growing to be harvested later for the winter hay. They crossed the bridge over Clear Creek where cool water flowed fast and deep from Blankenbuckler's spring. Then they climbed the hill to Yellow Plum Thicket and Old Clearing.

"Look at the berries, Mama! There are SO MANY! Why?"

"Years ago some early pioneer cleared out this little valley so he could farm it. Now it hasn't been plowed for several years, and it is growing back into forest. Look, already here and there you can see a clump of sumac or a tulip poplar or red oak growing up tall."

"The brambles are so high and deep, Daddy. How will we ever get to the berries?"

"Just follow me."

With his heavy boots he began to stamp and tramp down the bushes and weeds and berry canes to make a path so it would be easier for Mama and Ruth to follow and reach the berries inside the thicket. They followed the new narrow passageway Daddy had made. The berry brambles rose up high on both sides. It was like going into a tunnel without any roof. The berries hung on each side, just waiting for them. The bugs were thick too. Ruth was not afraid of the stinging insects flying around; she could watch out for spiders and their filmy webs that stuck to her face if she got caught in one. She didn't mind the butterflies and dragonflies and ants that came to sip the sweet juice, or the harmless little garter snakes resting in the brambles. She did try hard to chase away the giant horseflies; their bite was deep and burned fiercely. What she really tried to avoid were the shiny green stinkbugs. They did not sting or bite, but if you happened to grab one by mistake it made a dreadful stink in the air and on your fingers and it was very hard to get rid of the smell. It was miserable if you happened to taste a nice ripe berry that had a stinkbug nibbling on it; it took a lot of water to wash the rotten taste out of your mouth.

The sun seemed even hotter today, for the narrow valley did not let any breezes blow and even if the air stirred a little, it could not reach her in the tramped paths among the tall brambles. Her fingers were red and sticky from the berries; her hands were pricked from little thorns she could not avoid. She was hot and sweaty inside those miserable overalls. Fighting all those enemies really was hard work. Only the promise of the blackberry cobbler kept her from fussing.

By now they had tramped their way through brambles and brambles and brambles, and had almost reached the far end of Old Clearing. Suddenly Ruth looked up and saw something white, like smoke, rising above the trees from the other side of the hill.

"Is that a fire out here?"

Everybody stopped and looked.

"It's best we get out of here, quietly and quickly." They picked up their berry buckets and as noiselessly as possible retraced their way back through the paths they had tramped down earlier.

When they reached the open meadow, Daddy said in a low voice, "It's best we forget all about what we just saw. This could be very dangerous to us. Don't ever say a thing

"Is that a fire out here?"

about it. If anybody ever asks you, just tell them you didn't see anybody up there. This is very very important."

It was a big puzzle to Ruth. Why so much secrecy? Perhaps she would find out later.

At home, the first important job was to take a bath. Ruth scrubbed her body with brown Octagon soap, strong and powerful enough to kill any wicked chiggers which might have gotten to her bare skin through the coal oil on her overalls.

The next important job was to can the blackberries. Mama fired up the cook stove and put on her big feed sack apron. She put canning jars on to boil. Everybody sat down on the cool back porch to clean the berries, taking out leaves and trash. Mama put the clean berries in a pot on the stove.

While they were working the berries, Ruth had to know the secret of the mysterious smoke.

"Daddy, why aren't to tell anybody about the smoke we saw on The Forty?"

"Remember, we don't know anything. We didn't see anybody. But it could be some bootleggers have built a still on our Forty. Since there's nobody living there, they think they won't be discovered as the make moonshine."

"Why do they want to hide?"

"Eight years ago Congress made a new rule you can't drink liquor. But people want to drink it so much that they make it secretly. Such people are called bootleggers and the places where they make liquor are called stills. They cook mashed spoiled corn and draw liquor from it."

"So bootleggers are hiding on our farm, and don't want anybody to find them?"

"Now we don't know that they are; we didn't see them. Bootleggers are afraid that if somebody finds them, that person will report them to the revenuer—that's what they call the government officer. So if a revenuer finds them, they shoot him. If a person tells on them, they shoot him. If they even suspect a person may tell on them, they might shoot him. That's why it's very important that we never let anybody know what we saw."

"I won't tell anybody, Daddy. Not even Marie."

The canning job was terribly hot. When the berries boiled, Mama dipped the hot juice and fruit into clean glass jars that she had boiled and ready. She wiped the juice off the edge of the jar, screwed on the cap, and set the jar on a towel on the floor to cool. Often Mama had to wipe her face with her apron because she was dripping with sweat. If Ruth had to go into the kitchen, she scooted out very fast. She did not see how Mama could work in there.

But the best part was the cobbler Mama made for supper. She first rolled out pie crust and put one layer in the bottom of the cobbler pan. Then she put berries and flour and sugar over the crust, and another layer of crust on the top. She rarely used sugar for baking, so this was very special. She baked the pie in the oven while she worked over the hot stove.

That night, Mama brought that sweet cobbler to the table.

"Let's celebrate!" she said. "This is our reward for fighting all those bugs and thorns and the hot sun." They ate that berry cobbler, topped with rich cream skimmed from the milk crocks in the cellar. Each bite tasted better and better: sweet from the sugar, tangy from the good berries, flaky from the buttery crust, smooth from the cool cream. Ruth forgot how she had had to fight the pesky bugs and thorns and snakes, how she had had to be careful to avoid spider webs, stinkbugs, and trash in her bucket, how she had almost cooked inside those hot overalls, how her fingers had become sticky and pricked from the thorns, how she had endured the coal oil smell and the baking hot sun.

"Good, Little Peach?" asked Daddy.

"Yummy good!"

"Is it worth fighting all those enemies—the bugs and thorns and snakes and hot sun?"

"Oh, YES! I LOVE blackberry cobbler! It's wonderful! I don't even remember all the enemies now."

"Little Peach, that's the way heaven will be. So wonderful, we'll forget all the enemies we had to fight to get there. Let's have another piece of cobbler!"

"This is our reward for fighting all those bugs and hot sun."

CHAPTER 10

SNUG AS A BUG IN THE WOOD

FALL, 1928

Summer was closing down. The early peas and corn and green beans and cabbage were long ago finished. The fall vegetables, mustard and kale and collard greens, Chinese cabbage and turnips were still growing, and the tomato vines were still loaded with little green tomatoes. But most of the garden lay parched and brown. The last mowing of hay was safely packed into the open haymow above the cattle stalls.

One day when Marie came for water, she said, "Look at that woolly bear[1]. Let's ask it if it's going to be a hard winter." Ruth looked at a fuzzy caterpillar crawling as fast as it could on the ground.

"How can it talk to you?"

"'Course it doesn't really talk. You just look at the stripes and figure it out. See this one. The black stripes on each end are longer than that reddish stripe in the middle. That means a hard winter." Marie picked it up and it curled into a tight ball of bristles.

"Do they always tell the truth?"

"Well, I don't know. But that's what the old folks say."

When the maple trees were beginning to turn red and orange Mama had big news.

---

1   Woolly bear. Larva of a tiger moth (*Pyrrharctia Isabella*). They are bristly, with black stripes at each end and a reddish brown stripe in the middle. They curl into a ball when touched. Popular folklore claims that the size of the center stripe is a forecast of winter weather. In the fall they look for hiding places to winter over till spring when they make a cocoon from silk and their own hair. After two weeks they come out as a tiger moth. (Organic Gardening.com)

"It's time you had a room and bed of your own," she said. Up until now Ruth had slept in a little bed in one corner of the downstairs bedroom and her parents in the big bed in the opposite corner. "We're going to finish the little bedroom upstairs for you, and get you a big bed."

Daddy brought home a huge roll of gray felt paper. Mama bought wallpaper, cream colored with tiny pink roses sprinkled over it. First they unrolled the thick gray paper. Mama held it up to the unfinished walls, and Daddy nailed it on. The roughness and splinters were covered. Next Mama cooked paste with flour and water. They pasted the rose wallpaper on top of the gray paper. Ruth gazed at the transformation. Her room was the most beautiful one in the house. But more was to come.

"We're going to buy your bed today," said Mama. "We'll get it from Mrs. Williams."

Ruth had to watch Daddy hitch up the horses today, for this was very important business. He brought out Meg and Peg from the barn and they stood still in front of the wagon. They were fine horses, well trained. They would wait patiently to be hitched up and would not run away. He slipped the heavy collar around Meg's neck, and fastened her bridle to it, with the reins going all the way back to the driver's seat. He would guide Meg by pulling on one rein to show her which way to go. Next he put on her belly band and her traces, which he fastened to the wagon shafts so she could pull the load. Then he did the same for Peg.

It takes a long time to hitch up horses, especially when you are going to get your new bed. But it could not be done faster.

When they were harnessed, Daddy and Mama and Ruth climbed up the little step into the wagon and sat down on the long board seat. There was no back to lean against. Daddy said, "Giddy up!" and Meg and Peg set off up the road to Mrs. Williams house. They passed the Stubbs, the Websters, and the Coxes who had a springhouse full of milk crocks and water cress growing in the stream. They passed the long row of mailboxes where they picked up their mail once a week. The mailman would only come to Coxes house because the road further down to their house was too bad to travel on in the winter. Then they came to Mrs.Williams house, much like their own. Not a log cabin, but clapboard, weathered and gray.

Mrs. Williams came out to meet them. She wore a long dress with long sleeves, and a faded brown sweater over her feed sack apron. Her gray hair was done up on top of her head. She said,

"Bed frame's ready for you, out in the barn. Got a dresser to match. I'll throw it in too if you want to pay $7.00 for both the bed and the dresser."

Ruth held her breath. Would she get a dresser too? Yes, Daddy agreed to pay the extra $2.00. After the bed and dresser were loaded into the wagon, they went into the warm kitchen to pay her the $7.00 and visit awhile. Her kitchen table was covered with oilcloth[2] painted in nursery rhyme pictures. There was Jack and Jill going up the hill, Humpty Dumpty, and little Miss Mary eating her curds and whey.

They sat down around the shiny bright oilcloth table. Daddy gave Mrs. Williams the $7.00. "Paid $20.00 for the dresser and bed 25 years ago," she said. "I reckon I got $13.00 worth of use out of them when my kids were growing up."

The bent old woman got up from the table and opened the warming closet above the cook stove. She took out a fresh biscuit, spread it with honey and butter, and handed it to Ruth. Mama nodded her approval, and the girl took a bite of the sweet delicacy. It was light brown and crunchy on the outside. The inside was so soft and tender it seemed to just melt down on her tongue. She tried to make each bite last as long as she could. It was delicious, like blackberry cobbler.

"Thank you," she said.

---

2   Oilcloth. Cloth treated with oil or paint. Widely used for table and shelf coverings before plastic was invented. Could be wiped clean with a damp cloth.

"I want to give you something else, little girl. Here's a feather mattress for you. You'll need something to put on that bed to sleep on."

Ruth and Mama thanked her for the feather mattress.

After Ruth had eaten the last crumb of that wonderful biscuit, Mrs. Williams did something very strange. She took Ruth's little hand in hers, and said, "What beautiful hands you have!" Ruth had never imagined that her hands were beautiful. She looked at Mrs. Williams hands. They were wrinkled and shriveled and spotted and scarred with many years of use. She looked at her own little hands, tiny next to Mrs. Williams. Truly, hers were smoother and

Mrs. Williams looked at Ruth's hands.

newer with only dimples and no wrinkles. There was a great difference. Yes, her hands were beautiful!

"You are so right, Mrs. Williams," said Mama. "The older we get, the more wrinkled and bent and crippled and helpless we are. Won't it be wonderful when one of these days we can get new bodies in place of these worn out ones?"

"I never heard of a doctor that could do that! How does it work?"

"Well, the Bible says that when Jesus comes again He has promised to give us new bodies that will never get old again."

"You mean it actually says that?"

"Sure does. And Jesus is coming soon. All we have to do is get ready."

"I sure would like to get me a good new body."

"Would you like us to come up and read about it for you in the Bible?"

"Well, I guess I'll just ask my preacher about it. He will know all that."

Meg and Peg carried them back home and they unloaded the beautiful dresser and the wooden bed frames. Mama looked at the wood pieces and suddenly got very excited.

"Bed bugs!" she said. "Look in the crevices where the side boards are to fit into the headboard and footboard!"

Sure enough, inside the cracks tiny black bugs were crawling. They stood the wooden pieces up on the grass, and Mama got a bucket of hot water and Octagon soap and some rags and a brush. She scrubbed and rinsed, poured on boiling water, and scrubbed again until there was not a single crawly creature on that bed. Then they let the everything dry in the sunshine.

When the bed was dry, they carried the pieces upstairs and put the bed together. The oak headboard was decorated with a piece of molding across it, and so was the footboard. They fastened the two side frame pieces to the headboard and footboard, and laid the wooden slats across the bed. But how could she sleep on just wooden boards, Ruth wondered.

Mama said, "Tomorrow we will make your mattress." The next day Daddy hitched up Meg and Peg again and they drove up to the east field, next to Mt. Pisgah Baptist church. Mama brought out the mattress ticking she had made. It was like a huge pillowcase, open on one end. The field was full of dry sedges, standing prim and tall.

Daddy took his scythe out of the wagon. It had a wooden handle with a long curving blade fastened at an angle to one end. He swung his scythe, and the sharp blade cut the dry sedges. They fell down neatly in rows. Mama and Ruth gathered the dry grassy plants and stuffed them into the ticking. They stuffed and stuffed and packed and packed them down into that great ticking until it was so fat they could not stuff any more sedges in it. Then they drove Meg and Peg home.

Mama sewed up the open end of the ticking and the mattress was ready. They lugged and pulled and got it upstairs and put it on the slats of the new bed. On top of it Mama put the feather mattress Mrs. Williams had given Ruth. Next she put sheets, and a blanket, and her new crazy quilt she had just finished. The beautiful quilt was made of scraps of cloth cut in all kinds of shapes and sizes and sewed together without any pattern. It was tie quilted by taking single stitches of bright thread, tying them, and then cutting the ends. The seams were feather stitched, embroidered in red and blue. The bright colors of the patches and ties and feather stitching made a lovely bedcover that just cheered you up to look at it.

Ruth had to try it out. She climbed up on the high pile of the sedge mattress and feather mattress and quilts. She plunked down into the softness, smelling fresh like newly cut hay. When she moved it crunched and snapped. It was a good bed, a wonderful bed.

Ruth had always loved to sneak into her parents' bedroom when nobody was looking. She loved Mama's dresser. The curved wooden top of the mirror was carved, and the glass would swing back and forth. A white embroidered dresser scarf lay on the dresser and on it sat the mysteries. On one end was a round covered basket. Ruth would pick up the cover and gaze at the buttons inside. It must have contained every kind of button that could be made: all sizes, shapes, and colors. They could have made a great button string[3]. On the scarf lay Mama's cream colored ivory mirror and comb and brush to match. Mama said the ivory came from an elephant in Africa, so it was very expensive. She had paid $2.00[4] for the set when she was young lady, before she married Daddy.

Now Ruth had a marvelous dresser of her own, with a huge mirror, just like Mama's. She put on top of her new dresser her stereoscope and its magical cards. On the other end she put her box of sea shells that Aunt Julia had sent her in the mail from California. Mama had met Aunt Julia many years ago when she lived in Santa Monica. She was not a real aunt, but Mama's good friend. She had heard about Ruth, and had picked up those shells on the beach of the Pacific Ocean and sent them to Ruth. Now she had a wonderful dresser herself, complete with her own mysteries.

She put her doll Sophie on her chair in the corner next to her cedar table. Such an important day must be celebrated in some way. What should she do? Make a dress for Sophie! Of course! Never matter that she had never tried such a project. She asked Mama for a piece of flour sack and a needle and some of the embroidery thread she had used to feather stitch the crazy quilt.

Now just how do you make a dress? She would find out. She folded the cloth in half and cut a hole in the middle for Sophie's head to go through. She sewed up the sides, leaving just enough space for Sophie's cloth arms to go through. She threaded the needle in red and made a stitch through the cloth, tied it together and cut the ends. She made more red ties, then blue and pink and yellow and purple ones. She dressed Sophie in her new flour sack dress and set her back on her chair next to her cedar table.

---

3   Button string. In pioneer days varieties of buttons were hung on a string and used as a toy or decoration.

4   Dresser sets of mirror, comb, and brush made of ebony or fine porcelain, hand decorated in flowers and figures cost $1.75 to $2.25 in 1900. (Sears, Roebuck catalog)

She sat down in her own chair in front of the window, and looked out at the shrubs below. Ophelia had said they would be great for playing house, and she had been right. Marie had played with her many times there under the lilac and forsythia and mock orange and snowball bushes. She looked beyond the bushes to the creek garden where the angel had saved her life when she fell down in front of the harrow.

Her own room, papered with roses! Her own bed and her own mattress she had helped to make! No bugs in the bedstead either. And a celebration dress for Sophie!

They stuffed the dry sedges in the mattress ticking.

CHAPTER 11

PETE OLLICE

WINTER, 1928–1929

With the clean chimney the light would shine bright and clear.

Ruth knew they were well prepared for winter. Daddy had split plenty of firewood. The barn loft was stuffed full of fresh hay. He had heeled in the Chinese cabbage growing in the garden. Ruth watched him. First he dug a shallow pit in the garden and filled it with hay. Then he picked all the fat heads of Chinese cabbage, laid them on the hay, and covered them with more hay. Over the top he piled so much dirt it looked like an Indian mound. When they needed Chinese cabbage to eat or to take to market, he uncovered the soil and hay and there lay the crisp fresh heads. The cellar was full of potatoes and Mama's jars of canned food. There were plenty of dried apples and beans and kusha squashes too. In the garden were many winter greens which could stand frost and cold weather: mustard, turnips, kale, and collards.

There were winter chores to do even though the garden work was over. Every morning Daddy got up at four and milked the cows. Daddy also had to climb the ladder to the hayloft to pitch down hay for the animals. He fed them hay and cattle feed in their mangers. After breakfast he had to go out and turn the cattle and horses out and muck the stalls. Mucking was a stinky job. He always wore his high rubber boots in the barn and barnyard because the manure dropped by the animals was so sticky and nasty. To muck the stalls he raked up the dirty hay the animals had used the night before, and pitched it outside into a pile in the barnyard. This pile of hay and manure would compost and he would later spread it on the garden. Next he put in clean hay for bedding for the animals for the next night. The animals would stay out in the pasture all day and when they came home about four in the afternoon they would have a clean stall waiting for them. That was when he did the second milking, sitting on his little three legged stool and squeezing the teats of the cows so a steady stream of milk flowed into the milk bucket. Old Tom would come around for his share, and Daddy would squirt a stream into his mouth.

About four in the morning Mama first shook down the grate in the cookstove, and carried out the ashes. Then she started a fire to make breakfast. She stirred the coals in the fireplace, and started the fire there. She cooked a big vegetable breakfast. Perhaps she picked turnip greens from the garden, and cooked them, and baked potatoes and kusha squash in the hot oven. They would have a real farmer's breakfast with the vegetables and cottage cheese. They would eat the left-overs for the noon meal.

When Daddy brought in the buckets of milk, Mama poured it into the white milk crocks, through cheesecloth to strain out the trash.

One morning as they were eating their turnip greens and baked potatoes and kusha squash and cottage cheese, Mama said, "Churning day." So Ruth knew what her job was. After breakfast they gathered around the warm fireplace for morning worship. They sang, "He's the Lily of the Valley." Daddy read a short story from the Bible and prayed.

They were ready to work. Daddy went out to muck the barn. Mama carried up the crocks of clabbered milk from the cellar and poured the thick milk into her big iron pot. She heated it on the cookstove till it was barely warm, then she poured it into a clean feed sack and hung it from a peg on the end of the table. Under the sack she had put a dishpan to catch the clear whey that dripped through the sack. The clabber separated into curds. After three hours the whey had quit dripping and Mama scooped the snowy white cottage cheese out of the feed sack and into the jars that she would take to market.

While the whey was dripping, Mama took the cream she had skimmed from the top of the milk crocks the past few days, and poured it into the churn. Then Ruth put in the dasher. It was a long pole with two pieces of wood fastened crosswise over the bottom end. Over the pole she slid the lid, fitting its hole in the center right over the pole. Ruth sat beside the round wooden churn and raised the dasher up and down, up and down. The cream inside shook and chugged as she kept dashing and splashing. Every so often she carefully lifted the lid and peeked inside. Finally, when her arms were getting so tired she thought she could not churn another minute, she said, "Mama, butter!"

Mama skimmed the tiny yellow chunks out of the churn and mashed them together in the butter bowl. She washed and washed the butter till it was a solid golden ball and packed it into the round butter mold. When she took off the end later the round butter ball had a little flower on top. Today they would have all the buttermilk they could drink, so creamy and sour and good.

Ruth had regular chores too: helping carry in firewood and water and taking care of the fat Rhode Island and White Leghorn hens and roosters. The new baby chicks from the spring were grown up. All the chickens ran freely about the house and barnyard. Every afternoon Ruth carried them chicken feed and water and they ran and flew to her, squawking their welcome talk. The hens were different so she gave them names. Leonie, Dixie, Sue, and Ophelia. The chickens said, "Cawk, cawk, cawk, cawk."

"Cawk, cawk, cawk, cawk," said Ruth back to them. The more she talked, the more the chickens talked. After she gathered the eggs, and dusk began to fall, the chickens flew up into the apple trees beside the barn to roost on the branches for the night. But even though they roosted high above the ground, enemies sometimes found them. One night there was a fearful loud squawking from the direction of the barn. The next morning two hens lay dead, partly eaten, on the ground.

"Possums," said Daddy.

Another night there was again the terrified squawking When Daddy got up and tried to find out what was happening, he saw figures of two men running away from the barn. The next morning two hens were missing.

After thieves had stolen more chickens, Daddy said, "I'm going to build a chicken house, and a high fence around it. We'll keep the chickens inside at night where they will be safe."

The chicken house was safe, sometimes. Weasels still squeezed though the barred windows to suck the blood from the poor chickens, and people still managed to find ways to get in and steal.

One morning soon after Christmas, when Daddy planned to go to Oliver Springs, he came back inside without cranking up Lizzie.

"You won't believe this, but somebody has stolen a part from Lizzie again! They took her starter! She can't start!"

"How could that be? Lizzie is right outside our bedroom window!" said Mama.

"I did not hear any noise of any kind. They certainly were quiet. Well, that is the last time any thieves will steal parts from Lizzie," said Daddy.

"How are you going to keep Lizzie safe?" asked Ruth.

"We'll sell her. We can't supply Model T parts for free for anybody who wants them in Hen Valley."

"But Daddy, how will we take vegetables to Oliver Springs to sell?"

"With Meg and Peg hitched up to the buggy. We don't have to live like kings. We'll live just like the neighbors do."

That is how they said goodbye to faithful Lizzie and they never saw her again. It took much longer to drive the four miles to Oliver Springs with the horses than with Lizzie. But they saw more of their neighbors, passing slowly down Hen Valley Road. Most houses were log cabins, with smoke curling up from the stone chimney.

The logs were perched on a pile of smooth round stones at each corner for a foundation. The cracks were plastered with mud. Around the houses was a packed dirt yard, swept clean of leaves. A few houses had a shrub or two but almost none had any grass or flowers. The fields around the houses and barns were now stubby short cornstalks for the corn was all cut and shocked, and the ears themselves were stored in the corncribs, waiting to be shucked and shelled. Around the barns stood tall round haystacks, packed down around a tall pole and built so the rain water would run off. Cows were nibbling at the haystacks, eating their way into little sheltered overhangs and coves underneath the tall towers of hay. Several cabins had fenced in pigsties, which Ruth could smell even if she didn't see the pens or the pigs. Occasionally a few chickens ran about the barns and once in awhile a mule or horse or two also fed at the stacks. Seldom did they meet a car on the road, and almost never a team of horses and a wagon like they drove. Ruth always watched for the peacocks at the Harvey Hannah mansion.

Cows were nibbling their way into haystacks.

After Lizzie was sold, Pete Ollice dropped by one day. He wore bib overalls and denim cap and denim jacket, like most of the mountain men. He had a grizzled beard and grizzled hair and would look dangerous except his eyes were kind and gentle and his voice was soft.

"Hear you had bad luck with your Model T," he said.

"Yeah. Guess somebody thought they needed the parts worse than we did. But it won't happen again. Lizzie is gone."

"I'm sure sorry about them taking your parts like that. Hear they been taking your chickens too. "

"Yeah, lost quite a few chickens."

"Might get you some guinea hens. They won't let anything or anybody come by without making a fearful ruckus. Just like the peacocks that Harvey Hannah keeps at the mansion for watchdogs."

"I've been thinking of getting some guineas in the spring."

"That's good. The guineas will help. We shore do have some bad folks living in our valley. Did you hear what happened a few weeks ago to the Jedds?"

"No. What happened?"

"Well, the Jedds lived in the third holler down toward Elverton. They must have gone Christmas shopping in Olivers. While they were gone, one or two mean men snuck into their house and picked up everything they wanted. Then they sat down to eat the food they found. The Jedds came back home and the thieves killed 'em."

"Have the murderers been caught?"

"No way to find 'em. Folks think that mean Hank Scarborough was one of 'em but there's no way to prove it."

"Pete, I'm so sorry to hear about the Jedds. But, you know, I'm not surprised. This is one more sign that Jesus is coming soon."

"Really? What makes you think that Jesus is coming soon?"

"It's written down in the Bible. Says there, stealing and murders and all kinds of wickedness will get worse and worse before Jesus comes back."

"First time I ever heard such as that. Course I 'haint been to church in a long time."

"Pete, my family reads from the Bible every Saturday morning. We'd like you to come up and hear about it with us. We could read you about these signs that Jesus is coming soon. Could you come this next Saturday?"

"Sounds good. I believe I will. I'd like to hear more about these signs and stuff."

After Pete had gone, Daddy and Mama were smiling and happy.

"Pete sounded like he really wants to know more about Jesus coming," said Daddy.

"You were trying to plant joy seeds, weren't you?" said Ruth.

"You are right!"

Mama always scrubbed the floor on Fridays, but this Friday she knelt down and scrubbed extra well, till the floors were shiny. Pete Ollice was coming tomorrow! She dusted the furniture, and cleaned the coal oil lamps. She let Ruth lift off the glass chimneys and unscrew the wick holders. Mama poured more coal oil into the glass bowls and set the holders back on the bases. She turned the little screw at the side to make the wick turn higher. She let Ruth take the scissors and trim off the black top of the wide wick so it would burn clean and evenly. Next she washed in soapy water the glass chimneys which were blackened in spots where the flame had burned too high. With the clean chimneys the light would shine bright and clear. The lamps were ready for Sabbath.

Next was bath time in the kitchen. Mama set big pots of water on the cook stove to heat. When the water was hot, she poured it into the round tin washtub, and then added some cool water from the well. Ruth had first turn to use the bathwater. First she took off her dress and long white underwear and long black stockings. She had worn them for one week and now they would be washed. Mama had clean clothes for her to wear for the next week. Then she tested the water with her toe to be sure it was not too hot. Mama had a hot fire going in the cookstove, and had opened the oven door. Ruth could feel the good warmth coming from the oven. She stepped over into the tub and sat down in the good water. She could get all of herself in the tub if she curled her legs up tightly, but it was easier to put her legs over the edge of the tub. She wet her washrag and rubbed the brown Octagon soap over it. She would wash one leg at a time. The side of her next to the oven was very hot; the other side was wet and cold. When she dried off on the rough feed sack towel, she put on the clean underwear and clothes. Mama would use the water next, and Daddy last. Then they would carry that big washtub out on the porch and empty the water in the grass.

She could feel the good warmth coming from the stove.

They ate their usual supper of a bowl of whole wheat bread, broken up, with creamy milk poured over it, and some canned applesauce. It was the same supper they ate every day. But tonight it tasted special, for the bread was fresh and they each had an orange for a treat. The clean lamps shone brighter; the floor was brighter. The important day of rest and gladness had come as the sun set. It smelled good, it tasted good, it felt good.

They sat before the warm fire and began to sing Sabbath songs from "Christ in Song."

Don't forget the Sabbath,
The Lord our God hath blest,
Of all the week the brightest,
Of all the week the best;

It brings repose from labor,
It tells of joy divine,
Its beams of light descending,
With heav'nly beauty shine.

Welcome, welcome, ever welcome,
Blessed Sabbath-day.
Welcome, welcome, ever welcome,
Blessed Sabbath-day.

It felt good to have clean skin and clean clothes and be warm and singing happy songs. Ruth liked the happy Sabbath feeling on Friday night.

The next morning after feeding and milking the animals, and eating breakfast, they began looking for Pete Ollice. The living room was cheerful with the bright red blossoms on the amaryllis plants in front of the window, and the burning oak logs in the fireplace. Would Pete come?

Ruth saw him first. "He's coming!"

Daddy opened the front door and welcomed Pete to a rocking chair in front of the fireplace. "So glad to see you! Sit down and get warm. Right chilly today."

They talked some more. After awhile Daddy said, "We start our Bible reading with singing. Do you know the song, 'There's a Land That is Fairer than Day'?"

"I think I might have heard it once, when I used to go to church over in Elverton."

Daddy brought out his violin and tuned up. His bow flew back and forth across the strings in a sweet melody to lead the singing.

They sang "There's a Land That is Fairer Than Day", and "Shall we Gather at the River," and others. Then they prayed and began to read from the Bible. Daddy talked and talked and they read and read and Pete Ollice listened very intently. Ruth tried to listen but it was all grown up talk and it was hard to just sit there and be good. Usually when had their home Sabbath school, Mama read her Bible story for her, and for Marie, if she were there. Today everybody seemed to forget about Ruth. Finally she could stand it no longer, and said, "When are you going to have my story?"

Mama said, "Right now! Let's go into the kitchen." They sat down beside the warm cook stove and Mama said, "Sorry, we got so busy teaching Pete Ollice we forgot about you. We'll have your story now."

After the story, Ruth worked on memorizing her memory text, and repeated all the texts she had learned for the past two months.

After Daddy had finished the reading, Pete said, "Thanks, Mr. Rister. Them's powerful words you read. I can sure use good larning and need a lot more."

"So glad you liked them, Mr. Ollice. Please come again next Saturday."

After he left, Ruth said, "Will he come back again?"

"Don't know, Little Peach. Let's hope he will."

But Pete Ollice never came again for the Bible reading time. After several weeks passed, Ruth asked,

"Mama, do you think Pete Ollice did not like the joy seeds?"

"We don't know. Remember how when we planted a garden, some of the seeds did not come up, some got eaten by birds or rabbits, and bugs and pests ate on others?"

"I remember."

"It's the same way with growing joy seeds. There are many enemies to keep the good words from sprouting and growing in people's hearts. But we keep on planting. One day one seed, maybe more, will sprout and grow."

"And we'll be happy, and celebrate, just like we did with the blackberry pie when we finished picking berries!"

"You've got it!

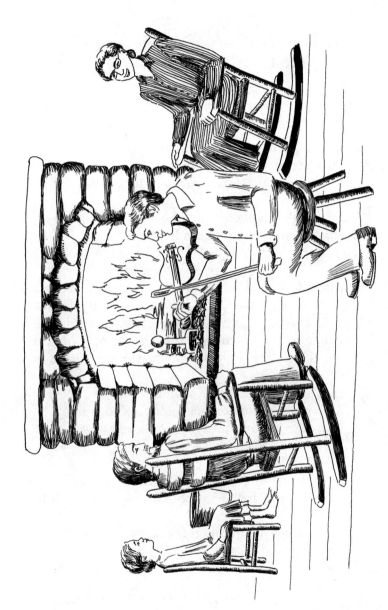

Daddy brought out his violin and tuned up.

CHAPTER 12

MYSTERIOUS VISITORS

1929

A Model T Ford pulled up in front of the house. A tall man in a brown suit and brown felt hat stepped out. His uniformed chauffeur, wearing a jaunty black billed hat, sat at the steering wheel. Daddy went out to greet the stranger. Ruth followed and hid behind the giant boxwood bushes on either side of the front steps.

"Hello! I'm Jeff McGregor," said the man.

"Hello, Mr. McGregor. I'm Knudt Risetter."

"My wife and I rode past your place on the train last week. She saw your two giant bushes in front of your house, and said they must be the biggest boxwoods in the world. I'd like to buy them as a present for my wife, to plant at our house in Knoxville. Would you be willing to sell them?"

"Never imagined anybody would want to buy our bushes. Well, how would you get them to Knoxville?"

"I'll send a truck and a crew of workmen to do the work. I'll give you $50.00 for the two shrubs."

"It's a deal. When will you come?"

"Next Wednesday I'll bring my crew and truck."

"Is that man going to take our boxwoods?" asked Ruth after the men left.

"Yes. I'm selling them to him for his wife."

"Oh." She looked at the giant bushes, so perfectly, smoothly round as if somebody had trimmed them. They were still green even now in the winter, when most trees and bushes were bare and brown. Truly, the boxwoods were beautiful. She had never thought about them before; just taken them for granted. And now they would be leaving. She would miss them.

The men dug out the giant boxwoods.

The following Wednesday Mr. Jeff McGregor returned with his chauffeur and truck with six men. They dug a circle around the first boxwood. As they dug deeper, they pushed burlap under the roots to make a great ball, which the men tied with ropes and then hoisted up into the truck. They did the same with the other bush.

When they were finished, Mr. McGregor handed over the $50.00.

Daddy said, "Thanks. And I have something else for you too." He handed Mr. McGregor a little leaflet. "Here's an idea that worth even more than the boxwoods."

"Thanks. I'll read it," said Mr. McGregor.

When the men had left, there were only gaping holes on either side of the porch where the giant bushes had stood. The house looked naked and cold without them. Daddy filled in the holes with dirt, but nothing would grow there from then on. But in her mind, Ruth could still see the biggest boxwoods in the world, cradling her house. Their beautiful memory would always live in her heart.

Other visitors came that spring, tiny ones. Not really visitors for they came to stay. Daddy ordered a box of baby guineas[1] for watchdogs. When he opened the lid, Ruth saw tiny brownish grayish balls of down running around inside the flat box. They looked something like baby chicks except they were smaller and had dark stripes running down their sides.

"They're so cute, but so tiny. How can they ever be watchdogs and chase thieves away?"

"Just wait till they grow up. They will scream so loudly nobody will dare to steal our chickens. They won't be as big as Harvey Hannah's peacocks but will scream just as frightfully."

One day another visitor came, a skinny scraggly cat. It was gray, not yellow like Old Tom, who had died during the winter. It meowed and meowed and tried to rub itself up against the legs of anyone who would stand still.

"Guess we better give it some milk," said Mama. She gave it a bowl of the fresh warm milk Daddy brought in that evening. The cat purred and purred and lay down on the porch on a pile of old rags. From then on, it drank milk every day and got fatter and fatter. A few weeks later it had four little naked, blind kittens. But they grew fast and soon were chasing each other back and forth, round and round the porch. Ruth loved to pull a string and watch them dash after it, or cuddle them in her arms, especially the little gray striped one with perfectly matched white paws. She named her Rosebud. Mr. Hickman had been right. Ruth did get her baby chicks and kittens. The farm really was fun!

Later another stranger knocked on the door.

"Hello!" the tall man said. "My name is Ed Banks. I have a great book for you!"

Daddy grinned from ear to ear. "By any chance, is your book called 'Daniel and Revelation'?"

"Yes, it is! But how did you know?"

[1] Guinea is a fowl smaller and lighter than a chicken. Belongs to the same family as the pheasant, but not as brightly colored. Has gray feathers, dotted with white. Lays tiny spotted eggs. Some people keep guineas for watchdogs, same as peacocks or geese. Originally came from Africa.

"I used to sell that book before we moved here. Do come in."

"Emma, come quickly!" called Daddy. "This is Brother Banks. He's selling the same book I used to sell!" Brother Banks shook hands with Emma.

"Is that your little girl hiding under the table?"

"Yes, that's little Ruth. She's a bit shy around strangers." Ruth peeked out at the man. He was so tall he had to bend over to get through the door. He wore a black suit and black felt hat. His hair and mustache were smooth and neatly trimmed. When he talked he smiled and his whole face seemed to glow.

"Hello, little girl," he said so kindly that Ruth knew she need not be afraid, but to be safe she stayed under the table just the same.

"We are so glad to see another Adventist! Where do you come from?"

"I live in Harriman and teach the church school there."

Do you mean there is a church in Harriman, with a school?"

"Yes, we have a church, just started in February last year, after Elder Wolfe held meetings the year before. How long have you lived here?"

"Almost a year and a half. We came in November of 1927."

"Where do you go to church?"

"Right here. We have home church every Sabbath."

"We'd love to have you come to church with us in Harriman."

"We'd love to, but must come by horse and buggy. How long will it take us to drive it?"

"It's about 12 miles, so it will probably take you about 3 or 4 hours."

"It will be a long trip, but we'll try it. You are just like finding family. We will be so glad to meet with other Adventists; it will be like having brothers and sisters again."

A big grin lighted up Daddy's usually solemn face, and Mama's too, as they waved goodbye.

The next Saturday afternoon a silvery blue Dodge touring car drove up and four strangers got out. Two were girls about the size of Ruth. The man wore a tan and white pin striped suit and tie and tan straw hat with a white band. His face was shaved clean so you could easily see his smile wrinkles. He stood tall and walked with strong strides. His voice was kind and cheery. The lady wore a navy blue flowered dress and navy blue straw hat to match. She walked with grace and elegance, holding herself erect like a queen. When she spoke her voice was like melodious bells in the distance.

"Is this where the Risetters live?" she asked.

"You've got the right place! Come in!"

"We're Grace and Gilbert Quinn, and these are our daughters, Patsy and Isabel."

Mr. Quinn tipped his hat and took it off. He said, "Brother Banks told us about you in church this morning, so we thought we'd look you up."

"What a treat to have an Adventist family visit us! I'm Knudt Risetter, and this is Emma and our daughter is Ruth."

The new girls were shy like Ruth so they did not talk to each other, but just listened to the grown-ups talk. Mrs. Quinn said she grew up in Graysville, where her family had moved to put their children in church school. Mr. Quinn managed his father's store in nearby Oakdale, the roundhouse[2] town.

Daddy took Mr. Quinn up to see the barn and garden with its tiny new onions and asparagus and peas bursting out of the ground. Mama took Mrs. Quinn to see the flowers. The forsythia bush was golden yellow. The mock orange was beginning to show its white buds, the lilac its purple buds, and the snowball its greenish buds. The wisteria vines on the front arbor were dripping with fuzzy

---

2 Turntable house to make an engine turn around. The engine stops on a round wooden platform. Then the entire platform begins to move. It circles around until the engine is headed in the opposite direction.

new leaves and long clumps of purple buds. The girls followed, saying very little.

Everybody went inside to talk. Mrs. Quinn told how several of her family in Graysville had been put into prison for working on Sabbath. One Sunday her father was out working where nobody could see him. He was in a back field stripping corn, not bothering anyone. Two men slipped out of their church, and sneaked up to spy on him. They asked him, "Don't you know this is Sunday?" He replied by quoting the fourth commandment. Two days later the sheriff arrested him and the others, including the president of Graysville school and her uncle and put them in prison. They were jailed for about a month. They had to work in a chain gang like criminals. She told about how happy she was to have a church in Harriman. Daddy told about their family secret, to plant seeds that would grow into a new church someday.

"You can help us plant seed in Harriman," said Mrs. Quinn. "We do so much want you to come help our church to grow."

"We'd like to, but it will be a long trip, driving the horses. We can't make it often."

"Do come when you can. We'll be looking for you. And please bring your violin."

After the visitors left, Ruth felt so happy, just as when Brother Banks had come. It was a special feeling, as though they had known each other for a long time. Was this what it would feel like to have brothers and sisters— to have a big family? She wondered if the church people in town would be like a family too. Brother Banks and the Quinns had so much to talk about, at least for the grown-ups.

A few weeks later Ruth's parents decided to try the twelve mile trip to Harriman. Daddy had to milk and feed the cows very early. Ruth had to get up early too. By six o'clock they climbed into the buggy and were off down Hen Valley road to Harriman. It was a bumpy ride, for the road had many potholes, washouts, and stones. Nobody else was traveling on the road.

After four hours they reached Harriman and found the church. Daddy fastened the horses to a post he found in the back. There were a few cars parked in front, but no other buggies.

When they entered, Mrs. Quinn was beaming, and said, "This is the Risetter family Brother Banks found out in Hen Valley! See, they ALL have red hair!" She told them the names of all those people: the Francises and Abstons and Jarnigans and Northerns and Mrs. Bazell and John Newell and old Tom Adkisson. Ruth felt afraid of all those grown ups, and she was glad to see Patsy and Isabel. They smiled at her and she smiled back. Brother Banks was not there. He had gone to North Carolina to visit his fiancé, Letah Scott.

Sabbath school began with songs and some other things. When it was time for the children's lesson, Somebody pulled a red velvet drape from each side and made a special room in the back for them. They sat in the desks used for church school.

Ruth liked the special part for the children, and wished they could come every week. Except one Sabbath. It was the end of the quarter. Mrs. Quinn asked Ruth to come to the front and repeat the thirteen memory verses she had learned during the last three months.

Ruth's legs felt like wet noodles but they took her up front to face all those people, looking at her and waiting for her to speak. She knew the verses perfectly; that was no problem. But all those faces were staring at her. Suddenly she had a great idea. In her pocket she carried her handkerchief, as everybody did. It was an important part of getting dressed in the morning. Your handkerchief had to be ready to wipe away the coughs and sneezes and sweat and tears. She took out her rumpled up dirty handkerchief and grasped one corner in one hand and the opposite corner in the other hand, making a swinging cradle. Then she lowered the swing to knee level, rested one knee in the hanky and began pulling the swing back and forth, back and forth. As she pulled, the fright melted away and she began fearlessly to repeat all thirteen of her verses, swinging her knee as she spoke.

She began pulling the swing back and forth, back and forth.

Later when they were home again, Daddy said, "Why did you swing your knee back and forth when you said your memory verses?"

"I don't know." She had no idea why. It was just the natural thing to do at that fearful moment. Daddy said no more, but somehow she knew she should never make a hanky swing again.

A few months later Brother Banks came back to their house, with his pretty wife Letah. She was tiny beside her giant husband. Her face seemed to shine with kindness when she smiled, which was often, like him. She wore a gorgeous golden brown dress which matched the curls framing her face. She must be the most beautiful lady in the world, thought Ruth, hiding under the table.

Brother Banks had come to borrow Meg and Peg to deliver his books. When Daddy hitched them up to the buggy, Letah Banks walked up; her husband took her arm and helped her put her foot on the high step into the buggy. Ruth watched every move and never forgot how kind Brother Banks was to his wife.

A few weeks after the Banks left, a package came in the mail, addressed to Ruth, from Letah Banks. Inside were new crayons and coloring book, new paper dolls and a celluloid[3] parrot. The bright red and yellow bird was sitting on a round celluloid perch which could swing from a string. Daddy hung the parrot just inside the dining room window, next to Ruth's favorite second stair seat. Every time Ruth looked at the celluloid bird, she remembered the most beautiful lady in the world. Someday she would be just like Letah Banks.

Brother Banks helped his wife up into the buggy.

---

3 Celluloid was invented by John Hyatt (1837–1920), who was trying to find a substitute for ivory to make billiard balls. He treated cotton fibers with chemicals to make a hard material which could be sawed, carved, and made into sheets. It was used to make combs, dentures, toys, and the first photographic roll film. Celluloid was the first synthetic plastic to be widely used. (World Book Encyclopedia)

CHAPTER 13

STOP THAT TRAIN

1929

That huffing wild engine spun off the railroad tracks in front of the house and ran straight toward Ruth. She was just outside her parents' bedroom when the monster began to chase her, puffing out terrible smoke and cinders and screaming at her. She began to run as fast as she could, but she had to look back to see if it was catching up with her. The giant hissed and whistled its blood curdling scream. It was getting closer and closer and began

The giant chased the poor girl round the house.

to chase the poor little girl around the house. Ruth knew there was no way she could outrun it. She screamed and woke up—in bed.

Over and over again she had this nightmare. Every day many trains passed the house, mostly slow freight trains, but twice a day the passenger train sped by very fast, once in the morning about 9:30 on its way from Knoxville to Chattanooga, and then again when it returned about 4:00 in the afternoon. The noise was deafening. If she were talking, she had to stop for nobody could hear her. Behind the engine was the coal car. The fireman shoveled coal from the coal car into the giant firebox, which burned and heated water which made steam to push the wheels around. The burning coal made clouds of black smoke and cinders; the steam made puffs of white which hissed and sizzled; the wheels on the engine and all the cars rattled and clacked over the rails. It still frightened Ruth even though she had lived there about two years now, and it was not just the noise that terrorized her, but something else, at night.

In the dark, trying to sleep, she remembered how twice thieves had stolen car parts from Lizzie in the night, right outside her parents bedroom window. She thought, perhaps the thieves did it when the trains were passing so they would not be heard. She remembered the chicken thieves came at night. She remembered Pete Ollice's story about the Jedds, and how somebody had killed them right in their own house. She thought of the unfinished room above their kitchen. It did not even have a window, just a great gaping space where a window was supposed to be. In the wintertime Daddy fastened over the open hole a window closer made of wood. But only a few wires held it in place. Anybody who wanted to could put a ladder up to the open space and come right into the upstairs—and the first person they would find would be Ruth, in her little bed. If that wicked person climbed up the ladder while the train was thundering past, and forced his way into her room, her parents could not hear her terrified screams, and then—what would happen to her? She lay down as small as she could in the bed, so such a person would not be able to even detect that anybody was there. Trains meant fear and terror.

One day Mama said, "I know a way we could save the long buggy rides to Oliver Springs with vegetables, and perhaps sell more too. I could go to Harriman on the morning passenger train and come back on the afternoon run."

"Are you sure the baskets would not be too heavy for you?" Daddy was concerned.

"You could help me carry the baskets to Scandlyn flag stop and stop the train. There are many more people in Harriman to sell to. You wouldn't waste all the time hitching up Meg and Peg and driving to Oliver Springs. You would have more time to work the gardens, and if you got tired, you could rest. I know I could do it. Let's try it."

Ruth said nothing, but shuddered inside. Daddy would stop that fearful monster that terrified her so much? Mama would actually ride in the train? Oh, no!

They did exactly that! On Monday morning her parents packed the market baskets as usual with vegetables and cottage cheese. But this time they stacked two baskets together and tied them with rope so Mama could carry two baskets tied together in each hand. They all walked the mile to Scandlyn together, Daddy carrying the heavy baskets. When they reached Scandlyn they set the baskets down in front of the station, a three sided building beside the railroad tracks. Soon they heard the train whistle for the flag stop. Daddy stood beside the tracks. When the engine rounded the bend, he waved his arm up and down.

The giant engine slowed, huffed and sizzled as a white cloud of steam puffed out around the enormous wheels. That huge frightening monster actually stopped for Mama! A nice man dressed in a blue uniform with gold buttons and a matching bill hat with gold braid stepped out of the passenger car and set down a stool. He helped Daddy lift the loaded baskets onto the platform that joined the cars, and he helped Mama climb up on the stool and the steep steps. Last of all the nice man picked up the stool, waved his hand to signal the engineer and yelled "All aboard!" Those eight giant wheels began to turn. The clouds of smoke and steam billowed out again. The train started up with a great jerk and jolt with Mama inside—off to Harriman.

All day Ruth wondered if Mama's plan was working. Was she able to carry those heavy baskets? Did she find new people who would buy her things? In the afternoon, she walked with Daddy to Scandlyn again to meet the four o'clock train. Just as it had in the morning, the monster engine slowed down with a grand huffing sizzling cloud of steam. The nice conductor again put down his little stepstool, tipped his hat to Daddy and Ruth, and helped Mama from the train, and her baskets too.

Ruth could hardly wait to find out what had happened.

"I sold everything—easy! Harriman Hotel is just one block from the train station. I took my baskets there first and sold some lettuce and onions and cottage cheese to the cook. I asked him if I could leave two baskets at the hotel while I sold vegetables in the town. He said he would see that they were safe. Then I carried the other two baskets up the hill — Cornstalk Heights they call it. There are lots of big fine homes on the hillside. The ladies came to the door; they were surprised and glad to see me. Sold out and had time to go the White Store and buy some salt and Crisco, and, Ruth, look at this!" She handed Ruth a small box with a picture of a girl carrying grapes on the front.

"Muscat raisins! Just like candy!"

Daddy was pleased the plan had worked out well; Ruth was pleased to get a special treat. That was the beginning of market days twice a week. Ruth began to be less afraid as she saw how kind the conductor was to Mama, and how friendly the engineer was. He would wave to them from his window seat high up in the cab of that fearful monster.

Very few country people flagged and rode the train, so the regular stop for Emma Risetter was unusual, but as it became a regular event, the engineer and conductor found out which house she lived in. As they became friends, these kind men saved their daily newspaper from Knoxville, tied it up in a tight roll, and began tossing it out at Ruth's house. It was fun to watch for the 9:30 train, see the engineer or fireman wave, and then toss out the newspaper roll. She waved back and ran to pick up the Knoxville Journal.

In the evenings they all sat in their rocking chairs around the fireplace and read about the world in those newspapers. Ruth heard her parents talk about the new president named Herbert Hoover. In October they read about a strange thing happening far away called a stock market crash[1]."

"The paper says a lot of people may be out of work after the crash," said Daddy.

"Sure thankful for our good farm and garden," said Mama. "We'll always have plenty of milk and eggs and vegetables and extra to sell."

"Yes, indeed. You know, we can really be thankful for my pellagra. It made us buy our wonderful farm and get settled here before this terrible crash came, and so many people may be out of work. It would be very hard to sell books now to people who have very little money for extras they can't eat or wear."

"The Lord is good. And you are feeling so much better with all this good milk and vegetables and eggs to eat."

"You are right. We could even say we are thankful for the pellagra now! We must never forget that God can work even unpleasant things together for good."

As Mama continued her market days twice a week, the trainmen began to be good friends of the family. One Monday the conductor said, "Mrs. Risetter, we have an idea to make your market days easier. Don't carry your heavy baskets the mile to the station. Take them out to the

---

1   Stock market crash October 24, 1929. Stocks lost six billion dollars in one day. In two years over 13 million people were out of work. The next five or six years were called the Great Depression.

front of your house and flag the train there like you do at Scandlyn. We'll stop for you. When we come back in the afternoon, we'll let you off at your house, too."

"Really? You'd stop the train at our house—just for me?"

"Yes, really. Try it next Thursday. We'll stop the train for you."

"Alright, I'll do it. How kind of you! Thank you very much!"

That is exactly what the kind train crew did from then on. Every Monday and Thursday morning the family stood at the railroad crossing in front of their house with the market baskets, loaded with vegetables. When the train chugged up the grade, Daddy waved his arm up and down just as he had at Scandlyn Station. The huge smoking steaming monster stopped, the nice man set down the stool for Mama, loaded on her baskets, and the train whistled and jerked and jolted and chugged off to Harriman. At 4:30 in the afternoon it stopped again and Mama got off the train, right in front of their houses. The engineer and fireman who ran the train became Ruth's friends. The dreadful noise didn't frighten her so much now. She didn't even notice when the freight trains passed—except at night when she was trying to go to sleep.

After she learned to read, she began to notice the names on the freight cars: Southern Railroad, Louisville and Nashville Railroad and others. One name she liked especially—Budweiser. It sounded so mysterious. When she played house she named her imaginary husband Budweiser, and called him Bud for short. She had no idea her "Bud" was the name of a beer. It was just a name on the nice trains that passed.

There was more. One day when Mama came home from selling her vegetables, she said, "Would you like to see a giant from the ocean—a whale[2]?"

---

2 Whales were once widely hunted for their layers of fat, or blubber, from which whale oil was made for lamps and cooking. When petroleum was found in the earth, people began to use kerosene instead and the whaling ships decreased. (Information on whales from World Book Encyclopedia)

Daddy waved his arm and the monster stopped in front of their house.

"You mean like the big fish that swallowed Jonah?"

"Exactly. Except we don't know for sure it was a whale that swallowed Jonah We know it WAS a big fish!!"

"How can I see it?"

"The train has brought some special cars to Harriman and left them on a siding. The whale is inside. I'll take you with me next market day to see it."

"Could Marie go see it too?"

"Why not? Let's ask her." But Marie's pa would not allow her to go on such an unheard of trip to Harriman.

So Ruth boarded that great monster herself and sat down with Mama on the softness of plush red velvet seats, wide enough for two people. Some seats were facing forward, and some backward. As the train jerked and began moving, the cloud of smoke and cinders floated back and some of it flew inside through the open window. She felt the clackety clack of the wheels as they passed over each rail joint. She looked up and saw the shine of polished wood walls and ceiling, with gold decorations along the luggage racks above the seats. She saw other people getting a drink at the end of the car. She tried it; she got a folded paper cup from the dispenser herself, opened it out, and got a drink by turning the spigot. She looked inside a little room at the end of the car behind the water fountain. There was a toilet with a tiny sink in the corner to wash. You sat on a seat with a hole underneath it that went straight down to the ground below. Ruth looked down through the hole, and could see the railroad ties and gravel whizzing by underneath. Now she understood why sometimes when she was walking on the railroad tracks, she saw toilet paper beside the rails. It had been dropped through the hole by somebody using the toilet.

In only a few minutes they reached Harriman and found the siding. There on a short railroad beside the regular tracks were two train cars hooked together. They bought tickets and stepped inside.

A man in uniform said, "Step right in folks, and see the biggest animal that has ever lived! You are about to see a baleen whale, caught in the Atlantic Ocean and preserved so you can see this wonder for yourselves. This whale is big enough so that the largest dinosaur ever found, and an elephant and a man, could stand together on top of it and still have lots of extra room."

Ruth saw the giant of a mouth, propped open so they could see the pink insides of its huge jaws.

"Look, Mama, no teeth! It looks like it eats with brushes!"

Another man in uniform said, "Those brushes are really long skinny bones, covered with bristles, called baleen. As the whale swims into a mass of small sea animals and plants, called plankton, it opens its mouth. Its giant tongue squeezes out the water through the baleen, and the whale swallows the plankton."

"How much plankton does it take for its dinner?" asked Mama.

"At least a half ton a day—probably more. You will notice that these baleen or whalebones[3], hang in two rows from the upper jaw. If any of you ladies wear corsets to tighten up the ugly bulges and make you have a beautiful figure, you probably wear whalebones to make the corset stiff. If you had lived back in the hoop skirt days, you might have worn whalebones for your hoops."

---

3   Whalebones or baleen, were used for women's corsets, bustles, and hoopskirts; also for buggy whips, umbrellas, fishing rods, etc.

Ruth stared at the giant mouth. She knew she could stand up inside it, behind the bristles, without bending over. She shuddered when she thought how Jonah must have felt when the great fish jaws closed over him and he slid down into its stomach and found himself in plankton slushing around inside. This whale would certainly have had a big enough stomach to hold a man.

Further down they passed a huge flipper, and finally the giant tail. Here another man explained that the tail fins, called flukes, are what the whale uses to swim. The flippers make it turn and balance.

He told them, "Under water it holds its breath and when it comes up for air, every 5 or 10 minutes, it blows out its breath in a very high spout like a fountain."

"Why doesn't a whale just stay out of the water on the beach if it breathes air?" asked someone in the group.

"If a whale gets stranded on a beach, it will die because it must have water to hold up its body and lungs. This one may weigh 150 tons. All this weight presses down on its lungs so it cannot breathe if it is out of water."

They passed along the back side of the mammoth whale. Then at the front of the car was another wonder— huge birds were standing tall and strutting round on ice. They were dressed smartly in black and white. Ruth loved neat birds, like the juncos and chipping sparrows in their cute little red hats. These tall birds certainly won the prize for a neat outfit. You could imagine they were on their way to church.

A man in uniform said, "These birds are penguins, from Antarctica. They cannot fly, so have to waddle around on their short legs. But with their flippers and webbed feet they can swim and dive very fast. They live most of their lives in the water, but do come on shore to lay their eggs and raise their babies. Sometimes as many as a million of them will huddle together to keep warm as they hatch and care for their babies."

When Ruth got home, Marie wanted to hear about the whale.

"You can't even imagine it! Our house would be too short to hold it. And the mouth! You and I could stand up together inside it! It's plenty big enough to have had a man inside it, like the Jonah story."

"Could you imagine Jonah getting caught by that big fish?"

"Yeah! And getting thrown out on the beach after three days!"

What marvels the train had brought! By now Ruth's fearful train enemies had become her friends. She just couldn't be afraid of the train any longer. And she was soon to find some entirely different friends, but they were not even in Hen Valley.

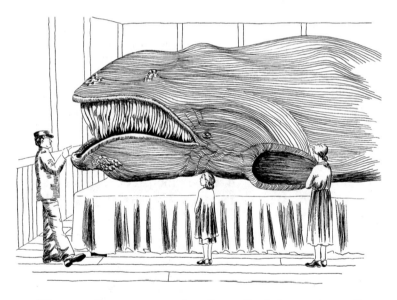

"You are about to see a giant from the Atlantic Ocean."

CHAPTER 14

TREASURE HUNT

1930

One Sabbath when Ruth and her family had gone to Harriman to church, she heard a very old man talking about a strange place called Coalfield but she forgot all about it. Daddy didn't forget.

"Little Peach, I'm going on a treasure hunt!"

"To find a buried treasure like in the story books?"

"Yes, sort of. Not buried, but forgotten!"

"You mean somebody had a treasure and now nobody knows where it is?"

"You've got it."

"Is it worth a lot of gold, like the pirate stories?"

"No. You can't sell it."

"What is it?"

"It's people! Forgotten people!"

"Oh, Daddy, people can't be treasures."

"Oh? You're my treasure. I've heard about some hidden forgotten people. They joined our church forty years ago and now nobody knows just where they are. So I'm going on a treasure hunt to find them."

"May I go too?" Ruth liked to ride along with her father on his trips to Cresses mill and store to get animal feed and coal oil. She loved sitting on the high wagon seat, wearing her starched blue dress and long bloomers to match, and hear him whistle as he drove the team down the road.

"Not this time. But if I find them I'll take you and your mother later."

A few days later Daddy hitched up Meg and Peg, and drove off in the buggy for Coalfield, taking a lunch and some books to sell. All day Ruth wondered if he was finding the treasure and what the strange people would be like. When he finally came home it was very late and already dark.

"Did you find the treasures?"

"Yes, I did! A lady who liked the Adventist preaching 40 years ago and still believes. She wants us to come and have Sabbath meetings with her and her daughter and grandchildren."

"Do I get to go too?"

"Of course. But it's a long way to drive the horses and buggy. I had to go to Oliver Springs, and then take a road through a gap in Walden's Ridge, and on about four more miles to Coalfield. It took so long that I think we can get there more quickly on our own feet."

"But we can't walk as fast as the horses can."

"Of course not. We'll take a shortcut—across Walden's Ridge."

"You mean, climb the mountain?"

"Exactly. Coalfield is just over Walden's Ridge from our house. I'll cut a trail and we'll hike across it."

The very next day Daddy took his axe over his shoulder and set off up the mountain to cut a trail. When he came back, he was pleased with his work.

"It's an easy trail. Only steep in one spot. We'll try it next Sabbath."

Early Sabbath morning they set out with a lunch, Bibles, and papers for the children. Daddy guided them up his new trail. From their pasture they followed the crest of a ridge that folded down from the mountain top, then rose higher and higher from the valley floor. When they reached the steep place, Ruth had to climb carefully so she would not slide back downhill. They found limestone cliffs near the top, with a narrow passageway they could climb through and come out on top of Walden's Ridge. She looked down from the top of the cliff. She could see little peeks of tiny houses far below and imagined she was a bird flying high and looking down at the world.

"There is an old old trail along the crest," said Daddy. "It's been made by Indians, trappers, and hunters for many years." They turned right on the Indian trail and walked until they found a charred tree stump.

"This is our marker to take the trail down the mountain."

"Looks like a black bear," said Mama. And so the black burned stump became the Black Bear ever after. They hiked down the opposite side of Walden's Ridge and came out in a clearing with a huge gray rocky mound in it.

"Shale from the old wagon mine that used to be here. Someday we'll stop and see it," promised Daddy.

They followed the wagon mine dirt road and came out on a better road.

"Is this Coalfield?"

"Not yet. This is Back Valley Road. We have to walk two more miles into town."

After another half hour they reached the village, much smaller than Oliver Springs. There were only a few houses and a railroad track.

"This is Coalfield, folks! But just wait till you see McCart's house." They crossed the railroad and a bridge. Just a bit further Ruth spied a high white house, set back from the road with a green lawn in front. It was tall, two stories high, with majestic white pillars holding up the front porch, so grand it reminded her of the Harvey Hannah mansion. Daddy led them right up to the beautiful house. "Now you will meet the treasures!"

Mae McCart met them with a big smile. She was short, with long hair coiled and wrapped around her head like a coronet. She was so happy that she greeted Daddy like he was a part of her family.

"Mrs. McCart, this is my wife Emma and my daughter Ruth."

"So glad to meet you all. Come in and rest. You must be tired—if you hiked over the mountain like you said you were going to do."

"Yes, we did hike over the mountain. I cut a trail during the week so it wasn't hard."

Three girls came in. "This is Billie, Betty and Bonnie. Billie, go get your grandma." The girls were quiet like Ruth and they just looked at each other without saying a word. Soon Grandma came from her house across the road.

"This is my mother, Minnie Davis. She was one of the members of the old church started forty years ago." Minnie Davis wore glasses and had long hair coiled on the back of her head. When she spoke her false teeth rattled in her mouth. But when she smiled, her face turned into a wreath of wrinkles and her eyes even smiled. "So glad you came back, Mr. Risetter, and brought your family, just like you said. We haven't had church for so long we've almost forgotten everything. Things just kind of fell apart at our old church when people moved away to the big church academy at Graysville."

They sat down in a circle of chairs in the McCart's living room.

"You are glad we came—but you have no idea how glad we are to come. You see, for years we've had a dream. We moved to Tennessee hoping to find people who wanted to learn to love God, and start a new church. So you are the beginning of that new church, in Coalfield. You are making our dream come true! You are real treasures!" Everybody smiled wide smiles. Even the shy girls were pleased to be part of the something special that was happening.

They started by singing some of the same songs they sang at home, and prayed. Then Mama took the four girls into the dining room and had their story and taught their memory text to them. She gave Billie, Betty, and Bonnie the children's papers she had carried over the mountain. Daddy stayed in the living room with the grownups and studied with them.

The girls loved the stories. "This is fun! Will you come again?"

"Yes, we will. Every Sabbath."

After the goodbyes, Daddy said, "I have another surprise for you. You cannot imagine where we're going to eat our picnic. Come with me."

They took the road back toward town, and walked over the bridge they had crossed earlier. "Now come down beside the creek." ·

They scrambled carefully down over the bank and the rocks below it. They heard water splashing. They looked up and saw water falling, a greater drop than McCart's house was tall. The creek dropped off a rocky ledge and its shining water tumbled wildly into a green pool below, white spray splashing up from the pool, and white foam piling up around the edges. This was much more exciting than the little creek Ruth loved to play in at home.

She paddled her hands in the water. Sleek minnows darted about. Little water striders skated over the quiet pools on the edge. Their air skate pads made round shadows below them on the sand. Mama spread out their picnic on a flat rock. Ruth had to carry her peanut butter and tomato sandwich with her so she could eat and explore at the same time. She clambered over the rocks to the opposite side of the pool and found dainty maidenhair ferns and mosses under the overhang there. A few feet below the pool the water tumbled over another ledge and splashed down in a second waterfall. The water was musical, singing as it dashed over the two falls.

"This is fun! Can we eat our picnic here every Sabbath?"

"Yes, indeed!" They rested a bit on the grass, soaking in the sounds of the singing, splashing falling water. Then they set out for the four mile hike back over the mountain. Ruth's legs were getting quite tired when they finally hiked back into the pasture clearing behind their house. Home looked so good. Their applesauce and bread and milk tasted much better than usual that night.

"Our special family secret is really coming true, isn't it?"

"It is indeed. Forty years ago somebody else planted the seeds." said Mama. "God has been watching over them all these years, and now they are sprouting."

"Are we going to hike the mountain every Sabbath?"

"Every week. It's going to take many more hikes over the mountain to keep the plants growing and sprout more. And God will help us! All you have to do is hike over the mountain with us every week and smile to everybody!"

"I can do that! That's easy."

The next week they hiked the mountain again, and the next. Then one day it rained. They had to wear galoshes over their shoes and carry umbrellas. Later on it snowed.

"Wear your sweater under your coat today, and your galoshes and mittens and a head scarf and neck scarf. You'll be toasty warm, wearing your long johns and black cotton stockings."

Ruth felt stuffed and tight in all the wrappings, but it was fun to slosh along the trail and see white caps covering even the scrubbiest bushes. The snow brightened and whitened and softened the hillsides.

One day Minnie Davis said, " Please visit my family who went to the little old church forty years ago. There are two sisters, cousins of my father-in-law, Joe Davis. They want to meet you."

Minnie gave directions to Artelia Adkisson's house, and the Risetters walked another mile to find her. She had heard about them and was happy to see them.

"Come in! So glad to have someone from our old church visit!"

After they were seated around the warm fire in the grate, Daddy began,

"I understand from Minnie Davis that you were one of the early Adventist believers, some forty years ago?"

"Yes, I was. I remember it like yesterday. Two strange men on horseback rode up to our house and sold us a book about Bible prophecy. My sister Lottie and I used to spend hours looking at the pictures of strange animals with wings and many heads."

"That's just what I used to do! Sold books for seven years. We called ourselves colporteurs. Tell me, did a preacher ever come?"

"Oh, yes, Preacher Scolls, in 1892 it was. I was just a little girl. My half-brother, John Davis, and my mother, and several others decided to follow his teachings. We had church every week. Then fifteen years later Preacher Byrd came. My half-brother, John Davis, started building a church in 1907 and we met in it even though it was not finished. But it was sad, so sad, the way, it turned out."

"What was so sad?"

"Well, the next year, 1908, John decided to move to the big Adventist center in Graysville to put his children in church school. Some of the others did too. Then the next year John died, and they brought his body home to bury here in Coalfield. But his widow, Mary Butler Davis still lives in Graysville. But when so many moved away, and we hardly ever had a preacher, our little group just went to pieces. Now we've just about forgotten everything."

"Good news for you!" said Daddy. "We're starting church again, in McCartt's house! So we can get pick up

Lottie and Artelia spent hours looking at the strange animals.

the pieces and add more! Tell us how to find your sister Lottie."

Ruth couldn't keep up with all the talk that went on and on. She kept busy looking at Artelia Adkisson's bun on the back of her head, and at the ferns on the lace panel curtains that hung at the windows, with heavy drapes beside them that made the room dark. She could just barely make out the massive picture frames that hung on the walls, holding dark pictures of solemn old people. On a small table stood a bouquet of waxed red paper roses.

Later Ruth and her family visited Lottie (Charlotte) Goddard, and her daughter, Theresa. They were just as happy as Telia Adkisson had been to know that their favorite church was starting up again at McCart's house.

Lottie Goddard told how long ago when she wsa a little girl, her mother had bought a Bible book from two book salesmen. She and her sister Artelia loved to look in the book at the weird animals with outrageous wings and horns. That unusual book made the family interested in the Bible and later they joined the new church.

On the way home Ruth asked her father about all the talk she couldn't understand.

"A long time ago, when your mama was only about two years old, two colporteurs came to Coalfield to sell books, just like I used to do. Remember when I used to come home with my book bag? I was so tired."

"And you just flopped down on the bed and slept all night."

"Right. These colporteurs sold Bible books to Artelia Adkisson's family. Then .a preacher came to Coalfield to tell more about the books, and several people believed and built a church."

"What happened to the church?"

"Many of the people moved away to Graysville, and things just fell apart. Artelia's half-brother died in Graysville. Her cousin, Lou went to the famous Battle Creek Sanitarium to take nursing, but she moved to California and died with her husband inside their house when it burned about eight years ago."

Ruth kept on hiking over the mountain. The little group in McCart's home grew. They all wanted to have a church again. They began to think of how to get more people to join with them, so Preacher Frank Harvey and his family came, to hold meetings.

"Aren't you the one that hikes over the mountain to come to the meeting?"

He pitched a tent in an open space near the house he had rented next to Artelia Adkisson's home. Ruth had never seen anything so strange as a cloth house with a sawdust floor. The cloth walls were rolled up and tied at meetings. Most of the other people in Coalfield were just as amazed as she was and they packed the wooden benches till there was no more room; then they stood outside the rolled up flaps of the tent. Everybody wanted to see the strange charts and pictures of weird animals with extra horns and heads and wings.

Many children crowded together on the front benches. Ruth was afraid, but one night she got brave enough to sit down next to one of the girls on the front bench, and even smiled at her. The girl smiled back and said,

"Aren't you the one that hikes over the mountain to come to meeting?"

"Yes, with my parents."

"Do you hike back again in the dark after the meeting?"

"That would be very hard to do! Pastor Harvey takes us home in his car."

"My name's Armethia. They call me Methia for short."

"My name's Ruth." From then on Ruth sat with Armethia every night. She learned the names of some of the other girls. There was Helen and Lois and Myrtle and Juanita and many others. They would smile when she came to sit with them and after awhile she was not afraid of them any more.

One night after Pastor Harvey had been preaching for three weeks, he said, "Several people have decided to become members of the new church. Saturday we will go to the falls and baptize them. Everyone is invited and welcome to come."

So the next Sabbath a group walked down to the blue green pool at the base of the falls. They carefully climbed down the bank and stood in a circle group and began singing "Shall We Gather at the River?" Armethia stood next to Ruth.

"Someday I want to be baptized like that."

Pastor Harvey walked right out into the water. Mae McCart followed him. He lifted his arm high and spoke, "Sister McCart, because you have accepted Jesus as Lord and Saviour of your life, I now baptize you in the name of the Father, the Son, and the Holy Spirit," and he lowered her down under the water and up again. Next followed Mrs. Goddard, and her daughter Theresa. Minnie Davis and Telia Adkisson joined the group of new members, but they had been baptized already so did not need to be baptized again. Pastor Harvey was smiling, the dripping wet new members were smiling, Daddy and Mama and Ruth were smiling along with the many others on the bank.

Then the preacher spoke again. "You are now newly adopted into the family of God. Thank God you have chosen to be part of the new Coalfield church!"

There was such a delightful happy spirit in the air, just like they were all in a special little group. Ruth thought it was the same cozy feeling as when Ed Banks came to visit, and the Quinns, and when they visited the church in

Harriman. Was this what it means to be part of a family? A church family? She whispered to Armethia, "Someday I want to be baptized like that to follow Jesus."

"Me too," Armethia whispered back.

That evening Mama made two of Ruth's favorites for a hot supper. She poached eggs in hot milk and served them on toast. She had even made rice pudding. "This has been a great day, and we must have something special tonight. But the great celebration is in heaven. The angels are having a real celebration for our friends who have chosen to be baptized today."

After they had eaten and were rocking in their comfortable chairs, Ruth said, "Our people are different."

"How, Little Peach? What do you mean?"

"Our church people are so happy. They just sound different when they talk; they act different, like they all belong together."

"You've got it! You see why for all these years we've talked and prayed about our special family secret—to start a new church. We wanted other people to have this same family spirit in their hearts and be happy too. And you have helped, hiking over the mountain every week, saying your memory verses and smiling to people at the meeting. I think you have already made some friends there in Coalfield. These young people may become members too. And you will help more and more as you grow older."

"Mama, something else."

"Yes?"

"Can I be baptized too?"

"Sure, when you are just a little older." Mama gave her a big hug.

Ruth thought to herself that it really was kind of like picking berries. Hiking over the mountain every week, getting wet and cold and tired and hungry, was something like fighting all the enemies when you picked berries. But it was worth it all when you tasted the delicious blackberry pie at the end of the long hot day. You forgot all the troubles when you tasted the sweet results.

We'd love to have you download our catalog of
titles we publish at:

www.TEACHServices.com

or write or email us your thoughts,
reactions, or criticism about this
or any other book we publish at:

TEACH Services, Inc.
254 Donovan Road
Brushton, NY 12916

info@TEACHServices.com

or you may call us at:

518/358-3494